HASKELL *from the very beginning*

In *Haskell from the Very Beginning* John Whitington takes a no-prerequisites approach to teaching the basics of a modern general-purpose programming language. Each small, self-contained chapter introduces a new topic, building until the reader can write quite substantial programs. There are plenty of questions and, crucially, worked answers and hints.

    Haskell from the Very Beginning will appeal both to new programmers, and to experienced programmers eager to explore functional languages such as Haskell. It is suitable both for formal use within an undergraduate or graduate curriculum, and for the interested amateur.

JOHN WHITINGTON founded a company which sells software for document processing. He taught functional programming to students of Computer Science at the University of Cambridge. His other books include the textbooks *"PDF Explained"* (O'Reilly, 2012) and *"OCaml from the Very Beginning"* (Coherent, 2013), and the Popular Science book *"A Machine Made this Book: Ten Sketches of Computer Science"* (Coherent, 2016).

HASKELL

from the very beginning

John Whitington

COHERENT PRESS

COHERENT PRESS

Cambridge

Published in the United Kingdom by Coherent Press, Cambridge

© Coherent Press 2019

First published October 2019
Reprinted with corrections May 2020

A catalogue record for this book is available from the British Library

ISBN 978-0-9576711-3-3 Paperback

by the same author

PDF Explained (O'Reilly, 2012)
OCaml from the Very Beginning (Coherent, 2013)
More OCaml: Methods, Algorithms & Diversions (Coherent, 2014)
A Machine Made this Book: Ten Sketches of Computer Science (Coherent, 2016)

Contents

Preface

This book is based on the Author's experience of teaching programming to students in the University of Cambridge supervisions system. In particular, working with students for the first-year undergraduate course "Foundations of Computer Science", lectured for many years by Lawrence C. Paulson.

An interesting aspect of supervising students from a wide range of backgrounds – some with no previous experience at all, taking Computer Science as an additional subject within the Cambridge Natural Sciences curriculum, and some with a great deal of programming experience already – is the level playing field which the functional family of languages (like Haskell) provide. Sometimes, those students with least prior programming experience perform the best.

I have tried to write a book which has no prerequisites – and with which any intelligent undergraduate ought to be able to cope, whilst trying to be concise enough that someone coming from another language might not be too annoyed by the tone.

One caveat: most things in life are small and elegant, or large and unwieldy. Haskell, as practised, is in the unusual position of being large and elegant. This may be the first Haskell book you read, but it will probably not be the last.

Special note to those who have already written programs

When I was a boy, our class was using a word processor for the first time. I wanted a title for my story, so I typed it on the first line and then, placing the cursor at the beginning, held down the space bar until the title was roughly in the middle. My friend taught me how to use the centring function, but it seemed more complicated to me, and I stuck with the familiar way – after all, it worked. Later on, of course, when I had more confidence and experience, I realized he had been right.

When starting a language which is fundamentally different from those you have seen before, it can be difficult to see the advantages, and to try to think of every concept in terms of the old language. I would urge you to consider the possibility that, at the moment, you might be the boy holding down the space bar.

Acknowledgments

The book was improved markedly by the comments of the technical reviewer, Stephen Dolan. Helpful additional review was provided by Michał Gajda, Jim Stuttard, Stuart Kurtz, Krystal Maughan, David Feuer, Gregory Popovitch, Steven Leiva, Charles Parker, and Dirk Markert. Any remaining errors are due solely to the author.

Getting Ready

This book is about teaching the computer to do new things by writing *computer programs*. Just as there are different languages for humans to speak to one another, there are different *programming languages* for humans to speak to computers.

We are going to be using a programming language called **Haskell**. A Haskell system might already be on your computer, or you may have to find it on the internet and install it yourself. We will be using the Glasgow Haskell system. You will know that you have it working when you see something like this:

```
GHCi, version 8.6.1: http://www.haskell.org/ghc/  :? for help
Prelude>
```

Please make sure the version number is at least 8. Haskell is waiting for us to type something. Try typing 1 space + space 2 followed by the Enter key. You should see this:

```
GHCi:
Prelude> 1 + 2
3
Prelude>
```

Haskell tells us the result of the calculation. You may use the left and right arrow keys on the keyboard to correct mistakes and the up and down arrow keys to look through a history of previous inputs. To leave Haskell, give the :quit command, again followed by Enter :

```
GHCi:
Prelude> :quit
Leaving GHCi.
```

You should find yourself back where you were before. If you make a mistake when typing, you can use the arrow keys on your keyboard to edit the text. To abandon typing, and ask Haskell to forget what you have already typed, enter Ctrl-C (hold down the Ctrl key and tap the c key). This will allow you to start again.

We are ready to begin.

Chapter 1

Starting Off

We will cover a fair amount of material in this chapter and its questions, since we will need a solid base on which to build. You should read this with a computer running Haskell in front of you.

Consider first the mathematical expression $1 + 2 \times 3$. What is the result? How did you work it out? We might show the process like this:

$$1 + 2 \times 3$$
$$\implies \quad 1 + 6$$
$$\implies \quad 7$$

How did we know to multiply 2 by 3 first, instead of adding 1 and 2? How did we know when to stop? Let us underline the part of the expression which is dealt with at each step:

$$1 + \underline{2 \times 3}$$
$$\implies \quad \underline{1 + 6}$$
$$\implies \quad 7$$

We chose which part of the expression to deal with each time using the familiar mathematical rules. We stopped when the expression could not be processed any further.

Computer programs in Haskell are just like these expressions. In order to give you an answer, the computer needs to know all the rules you know about how to process the expression correctly. In fact, $1 + 2 \times 3$ is a valid Haskell expression as well as a valid mathematical one, but we must write $*$ instead of $\times$, since there is no $\times$ key on the keyboard:

```
GHCi:
Prelude> 1 + 2 * 3
7
```

Here, `Prelude>` is Haskell prompting us to write an expression, and `1 + 2 * 3` is what we typed (the Enter key tells Haskell we have finished our expression). We'll see what `Prelude` means later. Haskell responds with the answer `7`.

Let us look at our example expression some more. There are two *operators*: $+$ and $\times$. There are three *operands*: 1, 2, and 3. When we wrote the expression down, and when we typed it into Haskell, we put spaces between the operators and operands for readability. How does Haskell process it? First, the text we wrote must be split up into its basic parts: `1`, `+`, `2`, `*`, and `3`. Haskell then looks at the order and sort of the

1

operators and operands, and decides how to parenthesize the expression: $(1 + (2 \times 3))$. Now, processing the expression just requires doing one step at a time, until there is nothing more which can be done:

$$(1 + \underline{(2 \times 3)})$$
$$\implies \quad \underline{(1 + 6)}$$
$$\implies \quad 7$$

Haskell knows that $+$ refers not to 1 and 2 but to 1 and the result of 2×3, and parenthesizes the expression appropriately. We say the $\times$ operator has *higher precedence* than the $+$ operator. An *expression* is any valid Haskell program. To produce an answer, Haskell *evaluates* the expression, yielding a special sort of expression, a *value*. In our previous example, $1 + 2 \times 3$, $1 + 6$, and 7 were all expressions, but only 7 was a value. Here are some mathematical operators on numbers:

Operator	Description
$a + b$	addition
$a - b$	subtract b from a
$a * b$	multiplication

The $*$ operator has higher precedence than the $+$ and $-$ operators. For any operator $\oplus$ above, the expression $a \oplus b \oplus c$ is equivalent to $(a \oplus b) \oplus c$ rather than $a \oplus (b \oplus c)$ (we say the operators are *left associative*). Negative numbers are written with $-$ before them, and if we use them next to an operator we may need parentheses too:

```
GHCi:
Prelude> 5 * (-2)
-10
```

Of course, there are many more things than just numbers. Sometimes, instead of numbers, we would like to talk about truth: either something is true or it is not. For this we use *boolean values,* named after the English mathematician George Boole (1815–1864) who pioneered their use. There are just two boolean things:

```
True
False
```

How can we use these? One way is to use one of the *comparison operators*, which are used for comparing values to one another:

```
GHCi:
Prelude> 99 > 100
False
Prelude> 4 + 3 + 2 + 1 == 10
True
```

Here are the comparison operators:

Operator	Description
$a == b$	true if a and b are equal
$a < b$	true if a is less than b
$a <= b$	true if a is less than or equal to b
$a > b$	true if a is more than b
$a >= b$	true if a is more than or equal to b
$a /= b$	true if a is not equal to b

Notice that if we try to use operators with things for which they are not intended, Haskell will not accept the program at all:

```
GHCi:
Prelude> 1 > True

<interactive>:2:1: error:
    • No instance for (Num Bool) arising from the literal '1'
    • In the first argument of '(>)', namely '1'
      In the expression: 1 > True
      In an equation for 'it': it = 1 > True
```

Do not expect to understand the details of this error message for the moment. We shall return to them later on. You can find more information about error messages in Haskell in the appendix "Coping with Errors" on page 197.

There are two operators for combining boolean values (for instance, those resulting from using the comparison operators). The expression a && b evaluates to True only if expressions a and b both evaluate to True. The expression a || b evaluates to True if a evaluates to True or b evaluates to True, or both do. In each case, the expression a will be tested first – the second may not need to be tested at all. The && operator (pronounced "and") is of higher precedence than the || operator (pronounced "or"), so a && b || c is the same as $(a$ && $b)$ || c.

We shall also be using *characters*, such as 'a' or '?'. We write these in single quotation marks:

```
GHCi:
Prelude> 'c'
'c'
```

So far we have looked only at operators like +, == and && which look like familiar mathematical ones. But many constructs in programming languages look a little different. For example, to choose a course of evaluation based on some test, we use the **if** ... **then** ... **else** construct:

```
GHCi:
Prelude> if 100 > 99 then 0 else 1
0
```

The expression between **if** and **then** (in our example 100 > 99) must evaluate to either True or False, and the expression to choose if true and the expression to choose if false must be the same sort of thing as one another – here they are both numbers. The whole expression will then evaluate to that sort of thing too, because either the **then** part or the **else** part is chosen to be the result of evaluating the whole expression:

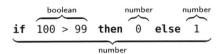

We have covered a lot in this chapter, but we need all these basic tools before we can write interesting programs. Make sure you work through the questions on paper, on the computer, or both, before moving on. Hints and answers are at the back of the book.

Questions

1. What sorts of thing do the following expressions represent and what do they evaluate to, and why?

   ```
   17
   1 + 2 * 3 + 4
   400 > 200
   1 /= 1
   True || False
   True && False
   if True then False else True
   '%'
   ```

2. These expressions are not valid Haskell. In each case, why? Can you correct them?

   ```
   1 + -1
   'A' == 'a'
   false || true
   if 'A' > 'a' then True
   'a' + 'b'
   ```

3. A programmer writes (1+2) * (3+4). What does this evaluate to? What advice would you give them?

4. Haskell has a remainder operator, which finds the remainder of dividing one number by another. It is written `rem`. Consider the evaluations of the expressions 1 + 2 `rem` 3, (1 + 2) `rem` 3, and 1 + (2 `rem` 3). What can you conclude about the + and `rem` operators?

5. Why not just use, for example, the number 0 to represent falsity and the number 1 for truth? Why have a separate True and False at all?

6. What is the effect of the comparison operators like < and > on alphabetic characters? For example, what does 'p' < 'q' evaluate to? What about 'A' < 'a'? What is the effect of the comparison operators on the booleans True and False?

So Far

1 Numbers ...-3 -2 -1 0 1 2 3...Booleans True and False. Characters like 'X' and '!'.

Mathematical operators + - * which take two numbers and give another.

Operators == < <= > >= /= which compare two values and evaluate to either True or False.

The "conditional" construct **if** *expression1* **then** *expression2* **else** *expression3*, where *expression1* evaluates to something boolean and *expression2* and *expression3* evaluate to the same sort of thing as one another.

The boolean operators && and || which allow us to build compound boolean expressions. The remainder operator `rem`.

Chapter 2

Names and Functions

So far we have built only tiny toy programs. To build bigger ones, we need to be able to name things so as to refer to them later. We also need to write expressions whose result depends upon one or more other things. Before, if we wished to use a sub-expression twice or more in a single expression, we had to type it multiple times:

```
GHCi:
Prelude> 200 * 200 * 200
8000000
```

Instead, we can define our own name to stand for the expression, and then use the name as we please:

```
GHCi:
Prelude> x = 200
Prelude> x * x * x
8000000
```

To write this all in a single expression, we can use the **let** ... = ... **in** ... construct:

```
GHCi:
Prelude> let x = 200 in x * x * x
8000000
Prelude> let a = 500 in (let b = a * a in a + b)
250500
Prelude> let a = 500 in let b = a * a in a + b
250500
```

We can use the special name it for the value resulting from the most recently evaluated expression, which can be useful when we forget to name something whilst experimenting:

```
GHCi:
Prelude> 200 * 200
40000
Prelude> it * 200
8000000
```

```
Prelude> it * 200
1600000000
```

The it name is not a part of the Haskell language – it is just a shortcut to make experimenting easier.

In Chapter 1, we talked about how values could be different "sorts of things" such as numbers and booleans and characters, but in fact Haskell knows about this idea – these "sorts of things" are called *types*, and every value and indeed every expression has a type. For example, the type of False is **Bool**. We can ask Haskell to tell us the type of a value or expression by using the :type command:

```
GHCi:
Prelude> :type False
False :: Bool
Prelude> :type False && True
False && True :: Bool
Prelude> :type 'x'
'x' :: Char
```

Note that commands like :type are not part of the Haskell language, and so cannot form part of expressions. We can read False && True :: Bool as "The expression False && True has type **Bool**". An expression always has same type as the value it will evaluate to. There is a further complication, which we shall only explain in detail later, but which we must confront on its surface now:

```
GHCi:
Prelude> :type 50
50 :: Num a => a
```

We might expect the type of 50 to be something like **Number** but it is the rather more cryptic **Num** a $\Rightarrow$ a. You can read this as "if a is one of the types of number, then 50 can have type a". In Haskell, integers and other numbers are sorts of **Num**. For now, we will not worry too much about types, just making sure we can read them without being scared. The purpose is to allow, for example, the expression 50 to do the job of an integer and a real number, as and when required. For example:

```
GHCi:
Prelude> 50 + 0.6
50.6
Prelude> 50 + 6
56
```

In the first line, 50 is playing the part of a real number, not an integer, because we are adding it to another real number. In the second, it pays the part of an integer, which is why the result is 56 rather than 56.0.

The letter a in the type is, of course, arbitrary. The types **Num** a $\Rightarrow$ a and **Num** b $\Rightarrow$ b and **Num** frank $\Rightarrow$ frank are interchangeable. In fact, Haskell does not always use a first. On the author's machine our example reads:

```
GHCi:
Prelude> :type 50
50 :: Num p => p
```

However, we shall always use the letters a, b etc. Let us move on now to consider *functions*, whose value depends upon some input (we call this input an *argument* – we will be using the word "input" later in the book to mean something different):

```
GHCi:
Prelude> cube x = x * x * x
Prelude> cube 200
8000000
```

We chose cube for the name of the function and x for the name of its argument. If we ask for its type, Haskell will reply by telling us that its type is **Num** a $\Rightarrow$ a $\rightarrow$ a. This means it is a function which takes a number as its argument, and, when given that argument, evaluates to the same sort of number. To use the function, we just write its name followed by a suitable argument. In our example, we calculated 200^3 by giving the cube function 200 as its argument.

The cube function has type **Num** a $\Rightarrow$ a $\rightarrow$ a, we gave it a number 200, and so the result is another number. Thus, the type of the expression cube 200 is **Num** a $\Rightarrow$ a (remember that the type of any expression is the type of the thing it will evaluate to, and cube 200 evaluates to 8000000, a number of type **Num** a $\Rightarrow$ a). In diagram form:

```
Num a ⇒ a → a    Num a ⇒ a
  ⎧‾‾‾‾‾‾⎫       ⎧‾‾‾‾⎫
    cube            200
  ⎩‾‾‾‾‾‾‾‾‾‾‾‾‾‾‾‾‾‾‾⎭
         Num a ⇒ a
```

It might be easier to see what is going on if we imagine missing out the part to the left of the $\Rightarrow$ symbol in each type:

```
  a → a      a
 ⎧‾‾‾‾⎫    ⎧‾‾⎫
   cube     200
 ⎩‾‾‾‾‾‾‾‾‾‾‾‾⎭
       a
```

If we try an argument of the wrong type, the program will be rejected:

```
GHCi:
Prelude>cube False

<interactive> error:
    • No instance for (Num Bool) arising from a use of 'cube'
    • In the expression: cube False
      In an equation for 'it': it = cube False
```

You can learn more about how to understand such messages in "Coping with Errors" on page 197. Here is a function which determines if a number is negative:

```
GHCi:
Prelude> neg x = if x < 0 then True else False
Prelude> neg (-30)
True
```

But, of course, this is equivalent to just writing

```
GHCi:
Prelude> neg x = x < 0
Prelude> neg (-30)
True
```

because x < 0 will evaluate to the appropriate boolean value on its own – True if x < 0 and False otherwise. What is the type of neg?

```
GHCi:
Prelude> neg x = x < 0
Prelude> :type neg
neg :: (Num a, Ord a) => a -> Bool
```

We can read this as "The argument to our function can have type a if a is an one of the class of types **Num** and also one of the class of types **Ord**. The result of the function is of type **Bool**". The class of types, or *typeclass* **Ord** is for things which can be ordered – in other words, ones on which we can use < and other comparison operators. A type which is one of a class of types is called an *instance* of that class. Here is another function, this time of type **Char** → **Bool**. It determines if a given character is a vowel or not:

```
GHCi:
Prelude> isVowel c = c == 'a' || c == 'e' || c == 'i' || c == 'o' || c == 'u'
Prelude> :type isVowel
isVowel :: Char -> Bool
Prelude> isVowel 'x'
False
```

The line is getting a little long. We can type a function (or any expression) over multiple lines by preceding it with : { and following it with : }, pressing the Enter key between lines as usual. Haskell knows that we are finished when we type : } followed by the Enter key. Notice also that we press space a few times so that the second line appeared a little to the right of the first. This is known as *indentation*.

```
GHCi:
Prelude> :{
Prelude| isVowel c =
Prelude|   c == 'a' || c == 'e' || c == 'i' || c == 'o' || c == 'u'
Prelude| :}
```

The start of the second line must be to the right of the name of the function: Haskell is particular about this. There can be more than one argument to a function. For example, here is a function which checks if two numbers add up to ten:

```
GHCi:
Prelude> :{
Prelude| addToTen a b =
Prelude|   a + b == 10
Prelude| :}
Prelude> addToTen 6 4
True
```

We use the function in the same way as before, but writing two numbers this time, one for each argument the function expects. The type is (**Eq** a, **Num** a) $\Rightarrow$ a $\rightarrow$ a $\rightarrow$ **Bool** because the arguments are both numbers, and both capable of being tested for equality (hence **Eq**) and the result is a boolean.

```
GHCi:
Prelude> :{
```

```
Prelude| addToTen a b =
Prelude|   a + b == 10
Prelude| :}
Prelude> :type addToTen
addToTen :: (Eq a, Num a) => a -> a -> Bool
```

Note that **Eq** and **Ord** are different. Not everything which can be tested for equality with == can be put in order with < and similar operators.

A *recursive function* function is one which uses itself. Consider calculating the factorial of a given number – the factorial of 4 (written $4!$ in mathematics), for example, is $4 \times 3 \times 2 \times 1$. Here is a recursive function to calculate the factorial. Note that it uses itself in its own definition.

```
GHCi:
Prelude> :{
Prelude| factorial n =
Prelude|   if n == 1 then 1 else n * factorial (n - 1)
Prelude| :}
Prelude> :type factorial
factorial :: (Eq a, Num a) => a -> a
Prelude> factorial 4
24
```

How does the evaluation of factorial 4 proceed?

$$
\begin{array}{ll}
 & \underline{\texttt{factorial 4}} \\
\Longrightarrow & 4 * \underline{\texttt{factorial (4 - 1)}} \\
\Longrightarrow & 4 * (3 * \underline{\texttt{factorial (3 - 1)}}) \\
\Longrightarrow & 4 * (3 * (2 * \underline{\texttt{factorial (2 - 1)}})) \\
\Longrightarrow & 4 * (3 * \underline{(2 * 1)}) \\
\Longrightarrow & 4 * \underline{(3 * 2)} \\
\Longrightarrow & \underline{4 * 6} \\
\Longrightarrow & 24
\end{array}
$$

For the first three steps, the **else** part of the **if** (or *conditional expression*) is chosen, because the argument a is greater than one. When the argument is equal to 1, we do not use factorial again, but just evaluate to 1. The expression built up of all the multiplications is then evaluated until a value is reached: this is the result of the whole evaluation. It is sometimes possible for a recursive function never to finish – what if we try to evaluate factorial (-1)?

$$
\begin{array}{ll}
 & \underline{\texttt{factorial (-1)}} \\
\Longrightarrow & -1 * \underline{\texttt{factorial (-1 - 1)}} \\
\Longrightarrow & -1 * (-2 * \underline{\texttt{factorial (-2 - 1)}}) \\
\Longrightarrow & -1 * (-2 * (-3 * \underline{\texttt{factorial (-3 - 1)}})) \\
 & \vdots \qquad \vdots
\end{array}
$$

The expression keeps expanding, and the recursion keeps going. You can interrupt this infinitely-long process by typing Ctrl-C on your keyboard (it may take a little while to work):

```
GHCi:
Prelude> factorial (-1)
^CInterrupted.
```

This is an example of a problem Haskell cannot find by merely looking at the program text – it can only be uncovered during the process of evaluation. Later in the book, we will see how to prevent people who are using our functions from making such mistakes.

One of the oldest methods for solving a problem (or *algorithm*) still in common use is Euclid's algorithm for calculating the greatest common divisor of two numbers (that is, given two positive integers a and b, finding the biggest positive integer c such that neither a/c nor b/c have a remainder). Euclid was a Greek mathematician who lived about three centuries before Christ. Euclid's algorithm is simple to write as a function with two arguments:

```
GHCi:
Prelude> :{
Prelude| gcd' a b =
Prelude|    if b == 0 then a else gcd' b (rem a b)
Prelude| :}
Prelude> gcd' 64000 3456
128
```

The function built-in function `rem` finds the remainder of dividing a by b. If we like, we can surround the function `rem` in backticks as `` `rem` `` (we have already seen this in Question 4 of the previous chapter). This allows us to put its two arguments either side, making it an operator like + and ||:

```
GHCi:
Prelude> :{
Prelude| gcd' a b =
Prelude|    if b == 0 then a else gcd' b (a `rem` b)
Prelude| :}
```

Here is the evaluation:

$$
\begin{array}{ll}
& \text{gcd' 64000 3456} \\
\Longrightarrow & \text{gcd' 3456 (64000 `rem` 3456)} \\
\Longrightarrow & \text{gcd' 1792 (3456 `rem` 1792)} \\
\Longrightarrow & \text{gcd' 1664 (1792 `rem` 1664)} \\
\Longrightarrow & \text{gcd' 128 (1664 `rem` 128)} \\
\Longrightarrow & \text{128}
\end{array}
$$

Why did we call our function `gcd'` instead of `gcd`? Because Haskell has a built in function `gcd`, and we should not reuse the name. Later on, when we load our programs from files, Haskell will in fact not let us reuse the name. This is another way in which Haskell is being rather careful, to prevent us being tripped up when writing larger programs.

Finally, here is a simple function on boolean values. In the previous chapter, we looked at the && and || operators which are built in to Haskell. The other important boolean operator is the `not` function, which returns the boolean complement (opposite) of its argument – `True` if the argument is `False`, and

vice versa. This is again built in, but it is easy enough to define ourselves, as a function of type **Bool** →
Bool.

```
GHCi:
Prelude> :{
Prelude| not' x =
Prelude|   if x then False else True
Prelude| :}
Prelude> :type not'
not' :: Bool -> Bool
Prelude> not' True
False
```

Almost every program we write will involve functions such as these, and many larger ones too. In fact,
languages like Haskell are often called *functional languages*.

A more formal look at types

Most readers will wish to skip this section, and the extra questions which relate to it, and not worry too much about types, coming back to it after a few more chapters have been worked through. However, for those who refuse to take things on trust without understanding them, it is perhaps best to tackle it now.

Every expression in Haskell has a *type*, which indicates what sort of thing it will eventually evaluate to. Simple types include **Bool** and **Char**. For example, the expression False || True has the type **Bool** because, when evaluated, it will result in a boolean value. So a type represents a collection of values. For example, the **Bool** type has two values: True and False, but the **Char** type has many more.

The purpose of types is to make sure that no part of the program receives something it was not expecting, and for which it cannot sensibly do anything. For example, the addition operator + being asked to add a number to a boolean. This avoids, at a stroke, a huge class of possible program misbehaviours, or bugs. Haskell can do this automatically, by working out the types of everything in the program and making sure they all fit together, and that no function can possibly receive an argument of the wrong type. This is called *type inference*, because the types are inferred (worked out) by Haskell.

When we ask Haskell what the type of 42 is, we get the surprising answer **Num** a $\Rightarrow$ a, rather than something simple like **Number**. The letters a, b, c... are *type variables* standing for types. A *typeclass* like **Num** is a collection of types. So, a typeclass is a collection of types, each of which is a collection of values. A type with a $\Rightarrow$ symbol in it has a left-hand and right-hand part. The left-hand part says which typeclasses one or more of the type variables on the right-hand side must belong to. So if 42 has the type **Num** a $\Rightarrow$ a we may say "Given that the type variable a represents a type which is an instance of the typeclass **Num**, 42 can have type a". Remember our example where a number was used as both an integer and a real number, even though it was written the same. Of course, many types do not have a $\Rightarrow$ symbol, which means either they are very specific, like **Bool**, or very generic, like a, which represents any type at all.

We have also introduced functions, which have types like $a \rightarrow b$. For example, if *a* is **Char** and *b* is **Bool**, we may have the type **Char** $\rightarrow$ **Bool**. Of course, functions may have a left-hand part too. For example, the function which adds two numbers may have the type **Num** a $\Rightarrow$ a $\rightarrow$ a $\rightarrow$ a. That is to say, the function will add any two things both of a type a which is an instance of the typeclass **Num**, and the result is a number of the same type.

So this is what is rather confusing to us about the type **Num** a $\Rightarrow$ a: it is actually rather harder to understand for the beginner than the function types in the previous paragraph, and yet it represents what we expect to be a simple concept: the number. All will be explained in Chapter 12.

We can have more than one constraint on a single type variable, or constraints on multiple type variables. They are each called *class constraints*, and the whole left hand part is sometimes called the *context*. For example, the type (**Num** a, **Eq** b) $\Rightarrow$ a $\rightarrow$ b $\rightarrow$ a is the type of a function of two arguments, the first of which must be of some type from typeclass **Num** and the second of some type from typeclass **Eq**.

Further complicating matters, sometimes every type of a certain typeclass is by definition also part of one or more other ones. In the case of the typeclasses we have seen so far, every type in the typeclass **Ord** is also in the typeclass **Eq**. What this means is that if we list the constraint **Ord** we need not also list **Eq**.

Questions

1. Write a function which multiplies a given number by ten. What is its type?

2. Write a function which returns `True` if both of its arguments are non-zero, and `False` otherwise. What is the type of your function?

3. Write a recursive function `sum'` which, given a number n, calculates the sum $1 + 2 + 3 + \ldots + n$. What is its type?

4. Write a function `power x n` which raises x to the power n. Give its type.

5. Write a function `isConsonant` which, given a lower-case character in the range `'a'...'z'`, determines if it is a consonant.

6. What is the result of the expression `let x = 1 in let x = 2 in x + x`?

7. Can you suggest a way of preventing the non-termination of the `factorial` function in the case of a zero or negative argument?

For those who are confident with types and typeclasses. To be attempted in the first instance without the computer.

8. Here are some expressions and function definitions and some types. Pair them up.

1	Ord a ⇒ a → a → **Bool**
1 + 2	(Ord a, Num a) ⇒ a → a → **Bool**
f x y = x < y	Num a ⇒ a → b → c → a
g x y = x < y + 2	Num a ⇒ a
h x y = 0	Num a ⇒ b → c → a
i x y z = x + 10	Num a ⇒ a

9. Infer (work out) types for the following expressions or function definitions.

Num a ⇒ a
Num a ⇒ a
```
46 * 10          2 > 1    Bool
f x = x + x      g x y z = x + 1 < y   (Ord a, Num a) ⇒ a → a → b → Bool
i a b c = b      a → b → c → b
```

10. Why are the following expressions or function definitions not accepted by Haskell?
```
True + False     No add on boolean
6 + '6'          types invalid
f x y z = (x < y) < (z + 1)   No Bool comparison for <
```

11. Which of the following types are equivalent to one another and which are different? Which are not valid types?

Num a ⇒ b ✗	Num t1 ⇒ t1
Num b ⇒ b → a	Num a ⇒ a → b
(Ord a, Num a) ⇒ a → a	Num a ⇒ a → a
(Num a, Ord a) ⇒ a → a	Num a ⇒ a

12. These types are correct, but have some constraints which are not required. Remove them.
```
(Eq a, Ord a) ⇒ a → b → a
(Ord a, Eq a, Eq b) ⇒ b → b → a
```

So Far

1 Numbers ...-3 -2 -1 0 1 2 3...Booleans `True` and `False`. Characters like `'X'` and `'!'`.

Mathematical operators + - * which take two numbers and give another.

Operators == < <= > >= /= which compare two values and evaluate to either `True` or `False`.

The "conditional" construct **if** *expression1* **then** *expression2* **else** *expression3*, where *expression1* evaluates to something boolean and *expression2* and *expression3* evaluate to the same sort of thing as one another.

The boolean operators && and || which allow us to build compound boolean expressions. The remainder operator `rem`.

2 Assigning a name to an expression using the *name = expression* construct. Building compound expressions using **let** *name1 = expression1* **in let** *name2 = expression2* **in** ...

Functions, introduced by *name argument1 argument2 ... = expression*. These have type $a \rightarrow b$, $a \rightarrow b \rightarrow c$ etc. for some types a, b, c etc. Recursive functions. Turning a two-argument function into an operator with backticks like `rem`.

The types **Bool** and **Char**. The typeclasses **Num**, **Ord**, and **Eq**. A function from values of type a to type b with a in typeclass **Eq** and b in typeclass **Ord** would have type (**Eq** a, **Ord** b) $\Rightarrow$ a $\rightarrow$ b.

The special value `it`. The command `:type` and the use of Ctrl-C to interrupt a computation.

Using Scripts

From now on, instead of showing the actual Haskell session...

```
GHCi:
Prelude> :{
Prelude| factorial n =
Prelude|   if n == 1 then 1 else n * factorial (n - 1)
Prelude| :}
```

...we will usually just show the program in a box, together with its type:

```
factorial :: (Eq a, Num a) ⇒ a → a

factorial n =
  if n == 1 then 1 else n * factorial (n - 1)
```

In fact, this is just how Haskell programs are normally written, in a text file with the .hs (haskell script) extension, rather than typed directly into Haskell. We can include the type in our .hs file, or leave it out and let Haskell infer it.

We can use the :load and :reload commands to access the program from Haskell. Assuming we have a file Script.hs which looks like the contents of the box above, we can use it like this:

```
GHCi:
Prelude> :load Script.hs
[1 of 1] Compiling Main             ( Script.hs, interpreted )
Ok, one module loaded.
*Main> factorial 24
620448401733239439360000
```

When we have made a change to the file Script.hs in our text editor (and saved the file), we can reload the new one:

```
GHCi:
*Main> :reload
[1 of 1] Compiling Main             ( Script.hs, interpreted )
Ok, one module loaded.
```

Chapter 3

Case by Case

In the previous chapter, we used the conditional expression **if** ... **then** ... **else** to define functions whose results depend on their arguments. For some of them we had to nest the conditional expressions one inside another. Programs like this are not terribly easy to read, and expand quickly in size and complexity as the number of cases increases.

Haskell has a nicer way of expressing choices – *pattern matching*. For example, recall our factorial function:

```
factorial :: (Eq a, Num a) ⇒ a → a

factorial n =
  if n == 1 then 1 else n * factorial (n - 1)
```

We can rewrite this using pattern matching:

```
factorial :: (Eq a, Num a) ⇒ a → a

factorial 1 = 1
factorial n = n * factorial (n - 1)
```

We can read this as "See if the argument matches the pattern 1. If it does, just return 1. If not, see if it matches the pattern n. If it does, the result is n * factorial (n - 1)." Patterns like n are special – they match anything and give it a name. Remember our isVowel function from the previous chapter?

```
isVowel :: Char → Bool

isVowel c =
  c == 'a' || c == 'e' || c == 'i' || c == 'o' || c == 'u'
```

Here is how to write it using pattern matching:

```
isVowel :: Char → Bool

isVowel 'a' = True
isVowel 'e' = True
isVowel 'i' = True
isVowel 'o' = True
isVowel 'u' = True
isVowel _ = False
```

The special pattern _ matches anything. If we miss out one or more cases – for example leaving out the final case, Haskell can warn us:

```
<interactive> warning: [-Wincomplete-patterns]
    Pattern match(es) are non-exhaustive
    In an equation for 'isVowel':
        Patterns not matched:
            p where p is not one of {'u', 'o', 'i', 'e', 'a'}
```

To enable this behaviour, you must start Haskell by writing ghci -Wincomplete-patterns instead of just ghci. Writing ghci -Wall enables all warnings. Haskell does not reject the program outright, because there may be legitimate reasons to miss cases out, but for now we will make sure all our pattern matches are exhaustive. Finally, let us rewrite Euclid's Algorithm from the previous chapter:

```
gcd' :: Integral a ⇒ a → a → a

gcd' a b =
  if b == 0 then a else gcd' b (a `rem` b)
```

Now in pattern matching style:

```
gcd' :: Integral a ⇒ a → a → a

gcd' a 0 = a
gcd' a b = gcd' b (a `rem` b)
```

We use pattern matching whenever it is easier to read and understand than **if** ... **then** ... **else** expressions.

What about this **Integral** typeclass? We did not try :type on the gcd' function in the last chapter, so we did not see this. A type of number which is an **Integral** has an additional property to one which is merely a **Num**, which is that whole-number division and remainder operations work on it. Since everything which is an **Integral** is also a **Num**, we do not see (**Num** a, **Integral** a), but just **Integral** a in the type.

Sometimes we need more than just a pattern to decide which case to choose in a pattern match. For example, in gcd' above, we only needed to distinguish between 0 and any other value of b. Consider, though, the function to determine the sign of a number, producing -1 for all numbers less than zero, 0 for just the number zero, and 1 for all numbers above zero:

```
sign :: (Ord a, Num a, Num b) ⇒ a → b

sign x =
  if x < 0 then -1 else if x > 0 then 1 else 0
```

We cannot rewrite this using a pattern match with three cases. Haskell has a facility called *guarded equations* to help us (each line in our pattern matched functions can also be called an equation). A *guard* is an extra check to decide if a case of a pattern match is taken based upon some condition, for example x < 0. Here is our sign function written using guarded equations:

```
sign :: (Ord a, Num a, Num b) ⇒ a → b

sign x | x < 0      = -1
       | x > 0      = 1
       | otherwise = 0
```

There is no need to line up the equals signs vertically, but we do so to make it easier to read. The cases are considered one after another, just like when using pattern matching, and the first case which matches the guard is taken. The **otherwise** guard matches anything, so it comes last. We use an **otherwise** case to make sure every possibility is handled. We can read the | symbol as "when". A function can be defined using multiple equations, each of which has multiple guarded parts.

The layout rule

We have mentioned indentation, noting that Haskell is particular about it. Indeed, programs will not be accepted unless they are properly indented:

```
GHCi:
Prelude> :{
Prelude| sign x =
Prelude| if x < 0 then -1 else if x > 0 then 1 else 0
Prelude| :}

<interactive> error:
    parse error (possibly incorrect indentation or mismatched brackets)
```

Haskell is telling us that it cannot work out what we mean. Since the **if** ... **then** ... **else** ... expression is part of the sign function, it must be indented further than the beginning of the whole sign expression. This applies at all times – even when the start of the whole expression is itself indented. In the case of **if** ... **then** ... **else** ... itself, it is in fact permitted not to indent:

```
GHCi:
Prelude> :{
Prelude| if 1 < 0
Prelude| then 2
Prelude| else 3
Prelude| :}
3
```

However, we shall often do so, when it is easier to read:

```
GHCi:
Prelude> :{
Prelude| if 1 < 0
Prelude|    then 2
Prelude|    else 3
Prelude| :}
3
```

Consider again our `sign` function:

```
sign :: (Ord a, Num a, Num b) ⇒ a → b

sign x | x < 0      = -1
       | x > 0      = 1
       | otherwise  = 0
```

We have already mentioned that lining up the equals signs is not necessary. However, we must always indent the cases. Here, we start the cases on the next line:

```
Prelude| sign x
Prelude|    | x < 0 = -1
Prelude|    | x > 0 = 1
Prelude|    | otherwise = 0
Prelude| :}
```

The layout rule is not complicated, but it can be frustrating to the beginner, especially when the error message is not clear.

Questions

1. Rewrite the `not'` function from the previous chapter in pattern matching style.

2. Use pattern matching to write a recursive function `sumMatch` which, given a positive integer n, returns the sum of all the integers from 1 to n.

3. Use pattern matching to write a function which, given two numbers x and n, computes x^n.

4. For each of the previous three questions, comment on whether you think it is easier to read the function with or without pattern matching. How might you expect this to change if the functions were much larger? Write each using guarded equations too.

5. Use guarded equations to write a function which categorises characters into three kinds: kind 0 for the lowercase letters a...z, kind 1 for the uppercase letters a...z, and kind 2 for everything else.

6. Experiment with the layout of the function definitions in this and the previous chapter. Which kinds of layout are allowed by Haskell? Which of the allowed layouts are aesthetically pleasing, or easy to read? Do any of your layouts make the program harder to change?

①
```
not' :: Bool -> Bool
not' True = False
not' False = True
```

②
```
sum' :: (Eq a, Num a) => a -> a
sum' n =
    if n == 1 then 1 else n + sum' (n-1)

sumMatch' :: (Eq a, Num a) => c -> c
sumMatch 1 = 1
sumMatch N = n + sumMatch' (n-1)
```

So Far

1 Numbers ...`-3 -2 -1 0 1 2 3`...Booleans `True` and `False`. Characters like `'X'` and `'!'`.

Mathematical operators `+ - *` which take two numbers and give another.

Operators `== < <= > >= /=` which compare two values and evaluate to either `True` or `False`.

The "conditional" construct **if** *expression1* **then** *expression2* **else** *expression3*, where *expression1* evaluates to something boolean and *expression2* and *expression3* evaluate to the same sort of thing as one another.

The boolean operators `&&` and `||` which allow us to build compound boolean expressions. The remainder operator `` `rem` ``.

2 Assigning a name to an expression using the *name = expression* construct. Building compound expressions using **let** *name1 = expression1* **in** **let** *name2 = expression2* **in** ...

Functions, introduced by *name argument1 argument2 ... = expression*. These have type $a \rightarrow b$, $a \rightarrow b \rightarrow c$ etc. for some types a, b, c etc. Recursive functions. Turning a two-argument function into an operator with backticks like `` `rem` ``.

The types **Bool** and **Char**. The typeclasses **Num**, **Ord**, and **Eq**. A function from values of type a to type b with a in typeclass **Eq** and b in typeclass **Ord** would have type (**Eq** a, **Ord** b) $\Rightarrow$ a $\rightarrow$ b.

The special value `it`. The command `:type` and the use of Ctrl-C to interrupt a computation.

3 Matching patterns using f *pattern1 = expression1* ↩ f *pattern2 = expression2* etc... The expressions *expression1, expression2* etc. must have the same type as one another. Writing functions using guarded equations like f x | *guard = expression* ↩ | *guard2 = expression2* | **otherwise** ... The typeclass **Integral**.

Chapter 4

Making Lists

A *list* is a collection of elements. Here is a list of three numbers:

```
[1, 2, 3]
```

We write a list between square brackets [and], separating the elements with commas. The list above has type **Num** a ⇒ [a], because it is a list of elements each of type **Num** a ⇒ a. All elements of the list must have the same type. The elements in the list are ordered (in other words, [1, 2, 3] and [2, 3, 1] are not the same list).

The first element is called the *head*, and the rest are collectively called the *tail*. In our example, the head is the number 1 and the tail is the list [2, 3]. So you can see that the tail has the same type as the whole list. Here is a list with no elements (called "the empty list" or sometimes "the nil list"):

```
[]
```

It has neither a head nor a tail. Here is a list with just a single element:

```
[5]
```

Its head is the number 5 and its tail is the empty list []. So every non-empty list has both a head and a tail. Lists may contain elements of any type: numbers, booleans, functions, even other lists. For example, here is a list containing elements of type **Bool**:

```
[False, True, False] :: [Bool]
```

Haskell defines two operators for lists. The : operator (pronounced "cons") is used to add a single element to the front of an existing list:

$$ \text{False : [True, False]} $$
$$ = \quad \text{[False, True, False]} $$

The cons operation is completed in a constant amount of time, regardless of the length of the list. The ++ operator (pronounced "append" or "concatenate") is used to combine two lists together:

$$ \text{[1, 2] ++ [3, 4, 5]} $$
$$ \Longrightarrow \quad \text{[1, 2, 3, 4, 5]} $$

This takes time proportional to the length of the list on the left hand side of the ++ operator (that is, a list of length 100 will take roughly twice as long as one of length 50). We will see why soon.

Now, how do we write functions using lists? We can use pattern matching as usual, with some new types of pattern. For example, here is a function which tells us if a list is empty:

```
isNil :: [a] → Bool

isNil [] = True                                                         the list is empty
isNil _ = False                                             it has at least one element
```

The argument has type [a] because this function does not inspect the individual elements of the list, it just checks if the list is empty. And so, this function can operate over any type of list. Functions like this are known as *polymorphic*. We can also use : in our patterns, this time using it to deconstruct rather than construct the list:

```
length' :: Num b ⇒ [a] → b

length' [] = 0                               the list has zero elements (the "base case")
length' (x:xs) = 1 + length' xs                            x is the head, xs the tail
```

The traditional name xs for the tail is pronounced *exes*. If two types are represented by the same letter they must have the same type. If they are not, they may have the same type, but do not have to. For example, in length', type a might happen to be in type class **Num** also, but it does not have to. Here is how the evaluation might proceed:

$$
\begin{aligned}
&\quad\ \text{length' [5, 5, 5]}\\
\Longrightarrow\ &\quad\ \text{1 + \underline{length' [5, 5]}}\\
\Longrightarrow\ &\quad\ \text{1 + (1 + \underline{length' [5]})}\\
\Longrightarrow\ &\quad\ \text{1 + (1 + (1 + \underline{length' []}))} \qquad \textit{base case}\\
\Longrightarrow\ &\quad\ \text{\underline{1 + (1 + (1 + 0))}}\\
\overset{*}{\Longrightarrow}\ &\quad\ 3 \qquad\qquad\qquad (\overset{*}{\Longrightarrow}\ \textit{means we are not showing all the steps})
\end{aligned}
$$

This works by recursion over the list, then addition of all the resultant 1s. It takes time proportional to the length of the list. Can you see why? Since x is not used in the expression 1 + length' xs, this function is also polymorphic. Indeed we can replace x in the pattern with the special pattern _ since there is no use giving a name to something we are not going to refer to:

```
length' :: Num b ⇒ [a] → b

length' [] = 0
length' (_:xs) = 1 + length' xs
```

A very similar function can be used to add a list of numbers:

```
sumElts :: Num a ⇒ [a] → a

sumElts [] = 0                          the sum of no elements is zero
sumElts (x:xs) = x + sumElts xs    otherwise, add the head to the sum of the tail
```

However, since we are actually using the individual list elements (by adding them up), this function is not as general – it operates over lists of type **Num** a ⇒ [a] only. Functions can, of course, return lists too. Here is a function to return the list consisting of the first, third, fifth and so on elements in a list:

```
oddElements :: [a] → [a]

oddElements [] = []                              the list has zero elements
oddElements [x] = [x]                            the list has one element
oddElements (x:_:xs) = x : oddElements xs   the list has more than one element
```

Consider the evaluation of oddElements [2, 4, 2, 4, 2]:

$$
\begin{array}{ll}
& \text{oddElements [2, 4, 2, 4, 2]} \\
\Longrightarrow & \text{2 : oddElements [2, 4, 2]} \\
\Longrightarrow & \text{2 : 2 : oddElements [2]} \\
\Longrightarrow & \text{2 : 2 : [2]} \\
\overset{*}{\Longrightarrow} & \text{[2, 2, 2]}
\end{array}
$$

You might notice that the first two cases in the pattern match return exactly their argument. By reversing the order, we can reduce this function to just two cases:

```
oddElements :: [a] → [a]

oddElements (x:_:xs) = x : oddElements xs    there is something to skip over
oddElements l = l                            there is nothing to skip over
```

We have seen how to use the ++ (append) operator to concatenate two lists:

$$
\begin{array}{ll}
& \text{[1, 2] ++ [3, 4, 5]} \\
\Longrightarrow & \text{[1, 2, 3, 4, 5]}
\end{array}
$$

How might we implement ++ ourselves, if it were not provided? Consider a function append xs ys. If the first list is the empty list, the answer is simply ys. But what if the first list is not empty? Then it has a head x and a tail xs. So we can start our result list with the head, and the rest of the result is just append xs ys.

```
append :: [a] → [a] → [a]

append [] ys = ys
append (x:xs) ys = x : append xs ys
```

Consider the evaluation of append [1, 2, 3] [4, 5, 6]:

$$
\begin{array}{ll}
& \underline{\text{append } [1, 2, 3] \ [4, 5, 6]} \\
\Longrightarrow & 1 : \underline{\text{append } [2, 3] \ [4, 5, 6]} \\
\Longrightarrow & 1 : 2 : \underline{\text{append } [3] \ [4, 5, 6]} \\
\Longrightarrow & 1 : 2 : 3 : \underline{\text{append } [] \ [4, 5, 6]} \\
\Longrightarrow & \underline{1 : 2 : 3 : [4, 5, 6]} \\
\stackrel{*}{\Longrightarrow} & [1, 2, 3, 4, 5, 6]
\end{array}
$$

This takes time proportional to the length of the first list – the second list need not be processed at all. What about reversing a list? For example, we want reverse' [1, 2, 3, 4] to evaluate to [4, 3, 2, 1]. One simple way is to reverse the tail of the list, and append the list just containing the head to the end of it:

```
reverse' :: [a] → [a]

reverse' [] = []
reverse' (x:xs) = reverse' xs ++ [x]
```

Here is how the evaluation proceeds:

$$
\begin{array}{ll}
& \underline{\text{reverse' } [1, 2, 3, 4]} \\
\Longrightarrow & \underline{\text{reverse' } [2, 3, 4]} \ ++ \ [1] \\
\Longrightarrow & \underline{\text{reverse' } [3, 4]} \ ++ \ [2] \ ++ \ [1] \\
\Longrightarrow & \underline{\text{reverse' } [4]} \ ++ \ [3] \ ++ \ [2] \ ++ \ [1] \\
\Longrightarrow & \underline{\text{reverse' } []} \ ++ \ [4] \ ++ \ [3] \ ++ \ [2] \ ++ \ [1] \\
\Longrightarrow & \underline{[] \ ++ \ [4] \ ++ \ [3] \ ++ \ [2] \ ++ \ [1]} \\
\stackrel{*}{\Longrightarrow} & [4, 3, 2, 1]
\end{array}
$$

This is a simple definition, but not very efficient – can you see why?

Two more useful functions for processing lists are take' and drop' which, given a number and a list, either take or drop that many elements from the list:

```
take' :: (Eq a, Num a) ⇒ a → [b] → [b]
drop' :: (Eq a, Num a) ⇒ a → [b] → [b]

take' 0 _ = []
take' n (x:xs) = x : take' (n - 1) xs

drop' 0 l = l
drop' n (_:xs) = drop' (n - 1) xs
```

For example, here is the evaluation for take' 2 [2, 4, 6, 8, 10]:

$$\text{take' 2 [2, 4, 6, 8, 10]}$$

$\implies$ 2 : take' 1 [4, 6, 8, 10]

$\implies$ 2 : 4 : take' 0 [6, 8, 10]

$\implies$ 2 : 4 : []

$\overset{*}{\implies}$ [2, 4]

And for drop' 2 [2, 4, 6, 8, 10]:

drop' 2 [2, 4, 6, 8, 10]

drop' 1 [4, 6, 8, 10]

$\implies$ drop' 0 [6, 8, 10]

$\implies$ [6, 8, 10]

Note that these functions contain incomplete pattern matches. The function fails if the arguments are not sensible – that is, when we are asked to take or drop more elements than are in the argument list. Later on, we will see how to deal with that problem. Note also that for any sensible value of n, including zero, take' n l and drop' n l split the list into two parts with no gap. So drop' and take' often appear in pairs.

Lists can contain anything, so long as all elements are of the same type. So, of course, a list can contain lists. Here is a list of lists of numbers:

[[1], [2, 3], [4, 5, 6]] :: **Num** a $\Rightarrow$ [[a]]

Each element of this list is of type **Num** a $\Rightarrow$ [a]. Within values of this type, it is important to distinguish the list of lists containing no elements

[] :: [a]

from the list of lists containing one element which is the empty list:

[[]] :: [[a]]

Other ways to build lists

Haskell provides a convenient shorthand for building useful lists of numbers by giving a starting point, and ending point, and perhaps one other. For example, we can write [1 .. 10] to define the list [1, 2, 3, 4, 5, 6, 7, 8, 9, 10]:

```
GHCi:
Prelude> [1 .. 10]
[1,2,3,4,5,6,7,9,10]
Prelude> [1, 3 .. 10]
[1,3,5,7,9]
```

We can use what is called a *list comprehension* to select and process elements from one list into another. For example, to calculate the list of squares of the numbers from 1 to 10:

GHCi:
```
Prelude> nums = [1 .. 10]
Prelude> [x * x | x <- nums]
[1,4,9,16,25,36,49,64,81,100]
```

We can read this as *"Each element of the list will be calculated using the expression x * x, where x is drawn from the list nums"*. More than one name can be assigned. For example, to produce a times table:

GHCi:
```
Prelude> [x * y | x <- [1 .. 5], y <- [1 .. 4]]
[1,2,3,4,2,4,6,8,3,6,9,12,4,8,12,16,5,10,15,20]
```

You can see that, in the case of multiple names, each later one cycles more quickly than the earlier one, so we have $x = 1, y = 1$ followed by $x = 1, y = 2$ rather than $x = 2, y = 1$. We can also specify *guards* to select and process only those items in the initial list which meet certain criteria. For example, to find all the even squares:

GHCi:
```
Prelude> [x * x | x <- [1 .. 20], x `rem` 2 == 0]
[4,16,36,64,100,144,196,256,324,400]
```

When we write a function involving the [..] construct, the type is different – it has an additional type constraint:

```
f : (Num a) ⇒ a → [a]
g : (Num a, Enum a) ⇒ a → [a]

f x = [1, x]
g x = [1 .. x]
```

The typeclass **Enum** includes such things as can be enumerated – that is to say, given one, we can find the next one. The integers, for example, are enumerable.

Lists of characters

A list of characters is special, and is called a *string*. It is printed between double quotation marks "like this". The types **String** and **[Char]** are interchangeable – it really is a list of characters, so we can use ordinary list functions:

GHCi:
```
Prelude> reverse' "stressed"
"desserts"
```

We will always write **String** instead of **[Char]** in our types for consistency.

Questions

1. Write a function `evenElements` which does the opposite to `oddElements`, returning the even numbered elements in a list. For example, `evenElements [2, 4, 2, 4, 2]` should return `[4, 4]`. What is the type of your function?

2. Write a function `countTrue` which counts the number of `True` elements in a list. For example, `countTrue [True, False, True]` should return 2. What is the type of your function?

3. Write a function which, given a list, builds a palindrome from it. A palindrome is a list which equals its own reverse. You can assume the existence of `reverse'` and the list concatenation operator ++. Write another function which determines if a list is a palindrome.

4. Write a function `dropLast` which returns all but the last element of a list. If the list is empty, it should return the empty list. So, for example, `dropLast [1, 2, 4, 8]` should return `[1, 2, 4]`.

5. Write a function `elem'` of type **Eq** a ⇒ a → [a] → **Bool** which returns `True` if an element exists in a list, or `False` if not. For example, `elem' 2 [1, 2, 3]` should evaluate to `True`, but `elem' 3 [1, 2]` should evaluate to `False`.

6. Use your `elem'` function to write a function `makeSet` which, given a list, returns a list which contains all the elements of the original list, but has no duplicate elements. For example, `makeSet [1, 2, 3, 3, 1]` might return `[2, 3, 1]`. What is the type of your function?

7. Can you explain why the `reverse'` function we defined is inefficient? How does the time it takes to run relate to the size of its argument? Can you write a more efficient version using an extra argument?

8. What are the lists `[1 .. 0]` and `[1, 2 .. 0]`? How might we make the list `[10, 9, 8, 7, 6, 5, 4, 3, 2, 1]`?

9. Use a list comprehensions to build a list of all positive numbers less than 10000 which have both 21 and 83 as factors, and the list which have either as factors.

10. Use a list comprehension to simplify your answer to Question 2.

So Far

1 Numbers ...-3 -2 -1 0 1 2 3...Booleans True and False. Characters like 'X' and '!'.

Mathematical operators + - * which take two numbers and give another.

Operators == < <= > >= /= which compare two values and evaluate to either True or False.

The "conditional" construct **if** *expression1* **then** *expression2* **else** *expression3*, where *expression1* evaluates to something boolean and *expression2* and *expression3* evaluate to the same sort of thing as one another.

The boolean operators && and || which allow us to build compound boolean expressions. The remainder operator `rem`.

2 Assigning a name to an expression using the *name* = *expression* construct. Building compound expressions using **let** *name1* = *expression1* **in** **let** *name2* = *expression2* **in** ...

Functions, introduced by *name argument1 argument2* ... = *expression*. These have type $a \rightarrow b$, $a \rightarrow b \rightarrow c$ etc. for some types a, b, c etc. Recursive functions. Turning a two-argument function into an operator with backticks like `rem`.

The types **Bool** and **Char**. The typeclasses **Num**, **Ord**, and **Eq**. A function from values of type a to type b with a in typeclass **Eq** and b in typeclass **Ord** would have type (**Eq** a, **Ord** b) $\Rightarrow$ a $\rightarrow$ b.

The special value it. The command :type and the use of Ctrl-C to interrupt a computation.

3 Matching patterns using f *pattern1* = *expression1* ↩ f *pattern2* = *expression2* etc... The expressions *expression1*, *expression2* etc. must have the same type as one another. Writing functions using guarded equations like f x | *guard* = *expression* ↩ | *guard2* = *expression2* | **otherwise** ... The typeclass **Integral**.

4 Lists, which are ordered collections of zero or more elements of like type. They are written between square brackets, with elements separated by commas e.g. [1, 2, 3, 4, 5]. If a list is non-empty, it has a head, which is its first element, and a tail, which is the list composed of the rest of the elements.

The : "cons" operator, which adds an element to the front of a list. The ++ "append" operator, which concatenates two lists together.

Using the : "cons" symbol for pattern matching to distinguish lists of length zero, one, etc. and their contents.

The shorthand list syntax [1 .. 10] and [1, 3 .. 10]. The typeclass **Enum**. List comprehensions [*expression* | *name* ← *list*, name2 ← *list2*, *guard*, *guard2*].

Strings, which are sequences of characters written between double quotes and are of type [**Char**] or **String**.

Two Ways of Thinking

Look again at our list appending function:

```
append :: [a] → [a] → [a]

append [] ys = ys
append (x:xs) ys = x : append xs ys
```

There are two ways to think about this computation. One way is to imagine the actions the computer might take to calculate the result:

Look at the first list. If it is empty, return the second list. Otherwise, pull apart the first list, looking at its head and tail. Return a list with the same head and whose tail is given by a recursive call to append the tail to the second list.

Alternatively, we can consider each match case to be an independent statement of truth, thinking the same way about the whole function:

The empty list appended to another list is that list. Otherwise, the first list is non-empty, so it has a head and a tail. Call them x and xs. Clearly append (x : xs) ys is equal to x : append xs ys. Since this reduces the problem size, progress is made.

It is very useful to be able to think in these two ways about functions you write, and to be able to swap between them in the mind with ease.

Chapter 5

Sorting Things

Lists often need to be in sorted order. How might we write a function to sort a list of integers? Well, a list with zero elements is already sorted. If we do not have an empty list, we must have a head and a tail. What can we do with those? Well, we can sort the tail by a recursive call to our `sort` function. So, now we have the head, and an already sorted list. Now, we just need to write a function to insert the head in an already sorted list. We have reduced the problem to an easier one.

```
sort [] = []                              an empty list is already sorted
sort (x:xs) = insert x (sort xs)          insert the head into the sorted tail
```

Now we just need to write the `insert` function. This takes an element and an already-sorted list, and returns the list with the element inserted in the right place:

```
insert :: Ord a ⇒ a → [a] → [a]

insert x [] = [x]                          the simple case – just put x in
insert x (y:ys) =                          otherwise we have a head and a tail
  if x <= y                                if we are at an appropriate point
    then x : y : ys                        just put x here
    else y : insert x ys                   otherwise, keep y and carry on
```

Consider the evaluation of `insert 3 [1, 1, 2, 3, 5, 9]`:

$$
\begin{aligned}
&\qquad\quad \underline{\texttt{insert 3 [1, 1, 2, 3, 5, 9]}} \\
&\Longrightarrow \quad \texttt{1 : } \underline{\texttt{insert 3 [1, 2, 3, 5, 9]}} \\
&\Longrightarrow \quad \texttt{1 : 1 : } \underline{\texttt{insert 3 [2, 3, 5, 9]}} \\
&\Longrightarrow \quad \texttt{1 : 1 : 2 : } \underline{\texttt{insert 3 [3, 5, 9]}} \\
&\Longrightarrow \quad \underline{\texttt{1 : 1 : 2 : 3 : 3 : [5, 9]}} \\
&\overset{*}{\Longrightarrow} \quad \texttt{[1, 1, 2, 3, 3, 5, 9]}
\end{aligned}
$$

Here are the workings of sort [53, 9, 2, 6, 19]. We have missed out the detail of each insert operation.

$$\begin{array}{ll}
& \text{sort } [53,\ 9,\ 2,\ 6,\ 19] \\
\overset{*}{\Longrightarrow} & \text{insert } 53\ (\text{sort } [9,\ 2,\ 6,\ 19]) \\
\overset{*}{\Longrightarrow} & \text{insert } 53\ (\text{insert } 9\ (\text{sort } [2,\ 6,\ 19])) \\
\overset{*}{\Longrightarrow} & \text{insert } 53\ (\text{insert } 9\ (\text{insert } 2\ (\text{sort } [6,\ 19]))) \\
\overset{*}{\Longrightarrow} & \text{insert } 53\ (\text{insert } 9\ (\text{insert } 2\ (\text{insert } 6\ (\text{sort } [19])))) \\
\overset{*}{\Longrightarrow} & \text{insert } 53\ (\text{insert } 9\ (\text{insert } 2\ (\text{insert } 6\ (\text{insert } 19\ (\text{sort } []))))) \\
\overset{*}{\Longrightarrow} & \text{insert } 53\ (\text{insert } 9\ (\text{insert } 2\ (\text{insert } 6\ (\text{insert } 19\ [])))) \\
\overset{*}{\Longrightarrow} & \text{insert } 53\ (\text{insert } 9\ (\text{insert } 2\ (\text{insert } 6\ [19]))) \\
\overset{*}{\Longrightarrow} & \text{insert } 53\ (\text{insert } 9\ (\text{insert } 2\ [6,\ 19])) \\
\overset{*}{\Longrightarrow} & \text{insert } 53\ (\text{insert } 9\ [2,\ 6,\ 19]) \\
\overset{*}{\Longrightarrow} & \text{insert } 53\ [2,\ 6,\ 9,\ 19] \\
\overset{*}{\Longrightarrow} & [2,\ 6,\ 9,\ 19,\ 53]
\end{array}$$

Here is the full program, known as *insertion sort*:

```
insert :: Ord a ⇒ a → [a] → [a]
sort :: Ord a ⇒ [a] → [a]

insert x [] = [x]
insert x (y:ys) =
  if x <= y
    then x : y : ys
    else y : insert x ys

sort [] = []
sort (x:xs) = insert x (sort xs)
```

Notice that the types have the **Ord** type constraint, because of the <= comparison operator in insert. Remember that Haskell's comparison functions like <= (used inside insert) work for any type which is an instance of typeclass **Ord**. For example, Haskell knows how to compare characters in alphabetical order, because the type **Char** is an instance of typeclass **Ord**:

$$\begin{array}{ll}
& \text{sort } ['p',\ 'i',\ 'm',\ 'c',\ 's',\ 'h'] \\
\overset{*}{\Longrightarrow} & ['c',\ 'h',\ 'i',\ 'm',\ 'p',\ 's']
\end{array}$$

How long does our sorting function take to run if the list to be sorted has n elements? Under the assumption that our argument list is unordered rather than sorted, each insert operation takes time proportional to n (the element might need to be inserted anywhere). We must run the insert function as many times as there are elements so, adding these all up, the sort function takes time proportional to n^2. You might argue that the first insert operations only have to work with a very small list, and that this fact should make the time less that n^2. Can you see why that is not true? What happens if the list is sorted already?

A more efficient algorithm can be found by considering a basic operation a little more complex than `insert`, but which still operates in time proportional to the length of the argument list. Such a function is `merge`, which takes two already sorted lists, and returns a single sorted list:

```
merge :: Ord a ⇒ [a] → [a] → [a]

merge [] l = l                          if the first is empty, just return the second
merge l [] = l                                                          and vice-versa
merge (x:xs) (y:ys) =
  if x < y
    then x : merge xs (y : ys)                   put x first because it is smaller
    else y : merge (x : xs) ys                                     otherwise put y first
```

When both lists are empty, the first case is picked because l matches the empty list. Here is how `merge` proceeds:

$$
\begin{array}{rl}
 & \text{merge } [9,\ 53]\ [2,\ 6,\ 19] \\
\Longrightarrow & 2\ :\ (\text{merge } [9,\ 53]\ [6,\ 19]) \\
\Longrightarrow & 2\ :\ 6\ :\ (\text{merge } [9,\ 53]\ [19]) \\
\Longrightarrow & 2\ :\ 6\ :\ 9\ :\ (\text{merge } [53]\ [19]) \\
\Longrightarrow & 2\ :\ 6\ :\ 9\ :\ 19\ :\ (\text{merge } [53]\ []) \\
\Longrightarrow & 2\ :\ 6\ :\ 9\ :\ 19\ :\ [53] \\
\overset{*}{\Longrightarrow} & [2,\ 6,\ 9,\ 19,\ 53]
\end{array}
$$

So merge can take two sorted lists, and produce a longer, sorted list, containing all the elements from both lists. So, how can we use this to sort a list from scratch? Well, we can use `length'`, `take'`, and `drop'` from the previous chapter to split the list into two halves. Now, we must use a recursive call to sort each half, and then we can merge them. This is known as *merge sort*.

```
mergeSort :: Ord a ⇒ [a] → [a]

mergeSort [] = []                                     we are done if the list is empty
mergeSort [x] = [x]                                 also if it has only one element
mergeSort l =
  let left = take' (length' l `div` 2) l                     get the left hand half
      right = drop' (length' l `div` 2) l                     and the right hand half
  in
    merge (mergeSort left) (mergeSort right)          sort sublists and merge
```

The `div` operator for integer division is used to halve the length (rounding down in the case of an odd-length list). The case for the single element is required because, if we split it into two halves, of length one and zero, the recursion would not end – we would not have reduced the size of the problem.

How does `mergeSort` work? Consider `mergeSort` on the list [53, 9, 2, 6, 19]. We will skip the inner workings of the `merge`, `drop'`, `take'`, and `length'` functions, concentrating just on `mergeSort` itself:

$$
\begin{array}{ll}
 & \texttt{mergeSort [53, 9, 2, 6, 19]} \\
\stackrel{*}{\Longrightarrow} & \texttt{merge (mergeSort [53, 9]) (mergeSort [2, 6, 19])} \\
\stackrel{*}{\Longrightarrow} & \texttt{merge (merge (mergeSort [53]) (mergeSort [9])) (mergeSort [2, 6, 19])} \\
\stackrel{*}{\Longrightarrow} & \texttt{merge (merge [53] (mergeSort [9])) (mergeSort [2, 6, 19])} \\
\stackrel{*}{\Longrightarrow} & \texttt{merge (merge [53] [9]) (mergeSort [2, 6, 19])} \\
\stackrel{*}{\Longrightarrow} & \texttt{merge [9, 53] (mergeSort [2, 6, 19])} \\
\stackrel{*}{\Longrightarrow} & \texttt{merge [9, 53] (merge (mergeSort [2]) (mergeSort [6, 19]))} \\
\stackrel{*}{\Longrightarrow} & \texttt{merge [9, 53] (merge [2] (mergeSort [6, 19]))} \\
\stackrel{*}{\Longrightarrow} & \texttt{merge [9, 53] (merge [2] (merge (mergeSort [6]) (mergeSort [19])))} \\
\stackrel{*}{\Longrightarrow} & \texttt{merge [9, 53] (merge [2] (merge [6] (mergeSort [19])))} \\
\stackrel{*}{\Longrightarrow} & \texttt{merge [9, 53] (merge [2] (merge [6] [19]))} \\
\stackrel{*}{\Longrightarrow} & \texttt{merge [9, 53] (merge [2] [6, 19])} \\
\stackrel{*}{\Longrightarrow} & \texttt{merge [9, 53] [2, 6, 19]} \\
\stackrel{*}{\Longrightarrow} & \texttt{[2, 6, 9, 19, 53]}
\end{array}
$$

From now on we will not be showing these diagrams all the time – but when you are unsure of how or why a function works, you can always write them out on paper yourself.

An alternative to **let** which some find more pleasing to read is the **where** construct, in which the main part of the code is given first, and the subsidiary definitions afterward.

```
mergeSort :: Ord a ⇒ [a] → [a]

mergeSort [] = []                                   we are done if the list is empty
mergeSort [x] = [x]                                 also if it has only one element
mergeSort l =
  merge (mergeSort left) (mergeSort right)          sort sublists and merge
    where
      left = take' (length' l `div` 2) l            get the left hand half
      right = drop' (length' l `div` 2) l           and the right hand half
```

How long does it take?

How long does merge sort take to run? We can visualize it with the following diagram, in which we have chosen a list of length eight (a power of two) for convenience.

```
[6, 4, 5, 7, 2, 5, 3, 4]
[6, 4, 5, 7][2, 5, 3, 4]
[6, 4][5, 7][2, 5][3, 4]
[6][4][5][7][2][5][3][4]
```

```
[4, 6][5, 7][2, 5][3, 4]
[4, 5, 6, 7][2, 3, 4, 5]
[2, 3, 4, 4, 5, 5, 6, 7]
```

In the top half of the diagram, the lists are being taken apart using `take'` and `drop'`, until they are small enough to already be sorted. In the bottom half, they are being merged back together.

How long does each row take? For the top half: to split a list into two halves takes time proportional to the length of the list. On the first line, we do this once on a list of length eight. On the second line, we do it twice on lists of length four, and so on. So each line takes the same time overall. For the bottom half, we have another function which takes time proportional to the length of its argument – `merge` – so each line in the bottom half takes time proportional to the length too.

So, how many lines do we have? Well, in the top half we have roughly $\log_2 n$, and the same for the bottom half. So, the total work done is $2 \times \log_2 n \times n$, which is proportional to $n \log_2 n$.

Questions

1. In `mergeSort`, we calculate the value of the expression `length' l `div` 2` twice. Modify the `mergeSort` function to remove this inefficiency.

2. We know that `take'` and `drop'` can fail if called with incorrect arguments. Show that this is never the case in `mergeSort`.

3. Write a version of insertion sort which sorts the argument list into reverse order.

4. Write a function to detect if a list is already in sorted order.

5. We mentioned that the comparison functions like < work for any Haskell type in typeclass **Ord**. Can you determine, by experimentation, how they work for lists? For example, what is the result of `[1, 2] < [2, 3]`? What happens when we sort the following list of strings of type **[String]** or **[[Char]]**? Why?

   ```
   [['o', 'n', 'e'], ['t', 'w', 'o'], ['t', 'h', 'r', 'e', 'e']]
   ```

6. Combine the `sort` and `insert` functions into a single `sortComplete` function, first using the **where** construct, then using the **let** construct instead.

So Far

1 Numbers ...-3 -2 -1 0 1 2 3...Booleans True and False. Characters like 'X' and '!'.

Mathematical operators + - * which take two numbers and give another.

Operators == < <= > >= /= which compare two values and evaluate to either True or False.

The "conditional" construct **if** *expression1* **then** *expression2* **else** *expression3*, where *expression1* evaluates to something boolean and *expression2* and *expression3* evaluate to the same sort of thing as one another.

The boolean operators && and || which allow us to build compound boolean expressions. The remainder operator `rem`.

2 Assigning a name to an expression using the *name = expression* construct. Building compound expressions using **let** *name1 = expression1* **in let** *name2 = expression2* **in** ...

Functions, introduced by *name argument1 argument2* ... = *expression*. These have type $a \rightarrow b$, $a \rightarrow b \rightarrow c$ etc. for some types *a, b, c* etc. Recursive functions. Turning a two-argument function into an operator with backticks like `rem`.

The types **Bool** and **Char**. The typeclasses **Num**, **Ord**, and **Eq**. A function from values of type *a* to type *b* with *a* in typeclass **Eq** and *b* in typeclass **Ord** would have type (**Eq** a, **Ord** b) $\Rightarrow$ a $\rightarrow$ b.

The special value it. The command :type and the use of Ctrl-C to interrupt a computation.

3 Matching patterns using f *pattern1 = expression1* ↔ f *pattern2 = expression2* etc... The expressions *expression1, expression2* etc. must have the same type as one another. Writing functions using guarded equations like f x | *guard = expression* ↔ | *guard2 = expression2* | **otherwise** ... The typeclass **Integral**.

4 Lists, which are ordered collections of zero or more elements of like type. They are written between square brackets, with elements separated by commas e.g. [1, 2, 3, 4, 5]. If a list is non-empty, it has a head, which is its first element, and a tail, which is the list composed of the rest of the elements.

The : "cons" operator, which adds an element to the front of a list. The ++ "append" operator, which concatenates two lists together.

Using the : "cons" symbol for pattern matching to distinguish lists of length zero, one, etc. and their contents.

The shorthand list syntax [1 .. 10] and [1, 3 .. 10]. The typeclass **Enum**. List comprehensions [*expression* | *name* ← *list*, *name2* ← *list2*, *guard*, *guard2*].

Strings, which are sequences of characters written between double quotes and are of type [**Char**] or **String**.

5 The `div` operator. The use of **where** as an alternative to **let**.

Chapter 6

Functions upon Functions upon Functions

Now would be an appropriate moment to go back to Chapter 2 and look at the extra material and questions on types and typeclasses, if you have not yet done so.

Often we need to apply a function to every element of a list. For example, doubling each of the numbers in a list. We could do this with a simple recursive function, working over each element of the list:

```
doubleList :: Num a ⇒ [a] → [a]

doubleList [] = []                                   no element to process
doubleList (x:xs) = (x * 2) : doubleList xs     process element, and the rest
```

For example,

$$
\begin{array}{rl}
 & \underline{\texttt{doubleList [1, 2, 4]}} \\
\implies & \texttt{1 * 2 : } \underline{\texttt{doubleList [2, 4]}} \\
\implies & \texttt{1 * 2 : 2 * 2 : } \underline{\texttt{doubleList [4]}} \\
\implies & \texttt{1 * 2 : 2 * 2 : 4 * 2 : } \underline{\texttt{doubleList []}} \\
\implies & \underline{\texttt{1 * 2 : 2 * 2 : 4 * 2 : []}} \\
\overset{*}{\implies} & \texttt{[2, 4, 8]}
\end{array}
$$

The result list does not need to have the same type as the argument list. For example, we can write a function which, given a list of numbers, returns the list containing a boolean for each: True if the number is even, False if it is odd.

```
evens :: Integral a ⇒ [a] → [Bool]

evens [] = []                                        no element to process
evens (x:xs) = (x `rem` 2 == 0) : evens xs     process element, and the rest
```

For example,

$$
\begin{array}{rl}
 & \underline{\text{evens [1, 2, 4]}} \\
\Longrightarrow & \text{False : } \underline{\text{evens [2, 4]}} \\
\Longrightarrow & \text{False : True : } \underline{\text{evens [4]}} \\
\Longrightarrow & \text{False : True : True : } \underline{\text{evens []}} \\
\Longrightarrow & \text{False : True : True : } \underline{\text{[]}} \\
\overset{*}{\Longrightarrow} & \text{[False, True, True]}
\end{array}
$$

It would be tedious to write a similar function each time we wanted to apply a different operation to every element of a list – can we build one which works for any operation? We will use a function as an argument:

```
map' :: (a → b) → [a] → [b]

map' f [] = []                                       no element to process
map' f (x:xs) = f x : map' f xs            process the element, and the rest
```

The `map'` function takes two arguments: a function which processes a single element, and a list. It returns a new list. We will discuss the type in a moment. For example, if we have a function `halve`:

```
halve :: Integral a ⇒ a → a

halve x = x `div` 2
```

Then we can use `map'` like this:

$$
\begin{array}{rl}
 & \underline{\text{map' halve [10, 20, 30]}} \\
\Longrightarrow & \text{10 `div` 2 : } \underline{\text{map' halve [20, 30]}} \\
\Longrightarrow & \text{10 `div` 2 : 20 `div` 2 : } \underline{\text{map' halve [30]}} \\
\Longrightarrow & \text{10 `div` 2 : 20 `div` 2 : 30 `div` 2 : } \underline{\text{map' halve []}} \\
\Longrightarrow & \text{10 `div` 2 : 20 `div` 2 : 30 `div` 2 : } \underline{\text{[]}} \\
\overset{*}{\Longrightarrow} & \text{[5, 10, 15]}
\end{array}
$$

Now, let us look at that type: $(a → b) → [a] → [b]$. We can annotate the individual parts:

$$
\underbrace{(a → b)}_{\text{function f}} \quad → \quad \underbrace{[a]}_{\text{argument list}} \quad → \quad \underbrace{[b]}_{\text{result list}}
$$

We have to put the function f in parentheses, otherwise it would look like `map'` had four arguments. This function can have any type $a → b$. That is to say, it can have any argument and result types, and they do not have to be the same as each other – though they may be. The argument has type [a] because each of its elements must be an appropriate argument for f. In the same way, the result list has type [b] because each of its elements is a result from f (in our `halve` example, a and b were both numbers in typeclass **Integral**). We can rewrite our `evens` function to use `map'`:

```
isEven :: Integral a ⇒ a → Bool
evens :: Integral a ⇒ [a] → [Bool]

isEven x = x `rem` 2 == 0

evens l = map' isEven l
```

In this use of map, type a was **Integral** a ⇒ a, and type b was **Bool**. We can make evens still shorter: when we are just using a function once, we can define it directly, without naming it:

```
evens :: Integral a ⇒ [a] → [Bool]

evens l =
  map' (\x -> x `rem` 2 == 0) l
```

This is called an *anonymous function*. It is defined using \, a named argument, the -> arrow and the function definition (body) itself. For example, we can write our halving function like this:

   \x -> x `div` 2

and, thus, write:

$$\text{map' (\textbackslash x -> x `div` 2) [10, 20, 30]}$$
$$\stackrel{*}{\Longrightarrow} \quad [5, 10, 15]$$

We use anonymous functions when a function is only used in one place and is relatively short, to avoid defining it separately.

In the preceding chapter we wrote a sorting function and, in one of the questions, you were asked to change the function to use a different comparison operator so that the function would sort elements into reverse order. Now, we know how to write a version of the mergeSort function which uses any comparison function we give it. A comparison function would have type **Ord** a ⇒ a → a → **Bool**. That is, it takes two elements of the same type in typeclass **Ord**, and returns True if the first is "greater" than the second, for some definition of "greater" – or False otherwise.

So, let us alter our merge and mergeSort functions to take an extra argument – the comparison function. The result is shown in Figure 6.1. Now, if we make our own comparison operator:

```
greater :: Ord a ⇒ a → a → Bool

greater a b =
  a >= b
```

we can use it with our new version of the mergeSort function:

$$\text{mergeSort greater [5, 4, 6, 2, 1]}$$
$$\stackrel{*}{\Longrightarrow} \quad [6, 5, 4, 2, 1]$$

```
merge :: (a → a → Bool) → [a] → [a] → [a]
mergeSort :: (a → a → Bool) → [a] → [a]

merge _ [] l = l
merge _ l [] = l
merge cmp (x:xs) (y:ys) =
  if cmp x y                                    use our comparison function
    then x : merge cmp xs (y : ys)              put x first – it is "smaller"
    else y : merge cmp (x : xs) ys              otherwise put y first

mergeSort _ [] = []
mergeSort _ [x] = [x]
mergeSort cmp l =
  merge cmp (mergeSort cmp left) (mergeSort cmp right)
    where left = take' (length' l `div` 2) l
          right = drop' (length' l `div` 2) l
```

Figure 6.1: Adding an extra argument to merge sort

In fact, we can ask Haskell to make such a function from an operator such as <= or + just by enclosing it in parentheses:

```
GHCi:
Prelude> :type (<=)
(<=) :: Ord a => a -> a -> a
Prelude> (<=) 4 5
True
```

So, for example:

$$\begin{array}{ll} & \text{mergeSort (<=) [5, 4, 6, 2, 1]} \\ \stackrel{*}{\Longrightarrow} & \text{[1, 2, 4, 5, 6]} \end{array}$$

and

$$\begin{array}{ll} & \text{mergeSort (>=) [5, 4, 6, 2, 1]} \\ \stackrel{*}{\Longrightarrow} & \text{[6, 5, 4, 2, 1]} \end{array}$$

Haskell provides a useful operator . to chain (or *compose*) functions together, so we may apply several functions to a value in order. For example, take the function double, we may write:

```
GHCi:
Prelude> double x = x * 2
Prelude> (double . double) 6
24
```

The effect is to quadruple the number. We can write the function directly if we like:

```
GHCi:
Prelude> quadruple x = (double . double) x
Prelude> quadruple 6
24
```

But, of course, we can drop the argument:

```
GHCi:
Prelude> quadruple = double . double
Prelude> quadruple 6
24
```

This can lead to cleaner, easier to read programs, once you are used to it. See how we can find two ways to quadruple each element in a list using `double` and `map`:

```
GHCi:
Prelude> (map' double . map' double) [6, 4]
[24,16]
Prelude> map' (double . double) [6, 4]
[24,16]
```

The `.` or function composition operator has type $(b \rightarrow c) \rightarrow (a \rightarrow b) \rightarrow a \rightarrow c$. That is to say we give it a two functions which, when used in order, take something of type a to something of type c via something of type b, and something of type a and we get something of type c out. In our examples, a, b, and c were all numbers. Since the function composition operator is associative, that is `f . (g . h)` is equal to `(f . g) . h`, we do not need the parentheses, and may write simply `f . g . h`, for example `times8 = double . double . double`. We may define the `.` operator ourselves:

```
GHCi:
Prelude> f . g = \x -> f (g x)
```

We can, in fact, write it like this too:

```
GHCi:
Prelude> (f . g) x = f (g x)
```

See how we define an operator just like a function, since in reality it is one. As another example, consider defining `+++` to mean vector addition:

```
GHCi:
Prelude> (a, b) +++ (c, d) = (a + c, b + d)
```

The techniques we have seen in this chapter are forms of *program reuse*, which is fundamental to writing manageable large programs.

Questions

1. Write a simple recursive function `calm` to replace exclamation marks in a string with periods. For example `calm "Help! Fire!"` should evaluate to `"Help. Fire."`. Now rewrite your function to use `map'` instead of recursion. What are the types of your functions?

2. Write a function `clip` which, given a number, clips it to the range 1 . . . 10 so that numbers bigger than 10 round down to 10, and those smaller than 1 round up to 1. Write another function `clipList` which uses this first function together with `map'` to apply this clipping to a whole list of numbers.

3. Express your function `clipList` again, this time using an anonymous function instead of `clip`.

4. Write a function `apply` which, given another function, a number of times to apply it, and an initial argument for the function, will return the cumulative effect of repeatedly applying the function. For instance, `apply f 6 4` should return `f (f (f (f (f (f 4))))))`. What is the type of your function?

5. Modify the insertion sort function from the preceding chapter to take a comparison function, in the same way that we modified merge sort in this chapter. What is its type?

6. Write a function `filter'` which takes a function of type a → **Bool** and an [a] and returns a list of just those elements of the argument list for which the given function returns `True`.

7. Write the function `all'` which, given a function of type a → **Bool** and an argument list of type [a] evaluates to `True` if and only if the function returns `True` for every element of the list. Give examples of its use.

8. Write a function `mapl` which maps a function of type a → b over a list of type [[a]] to produce a list of type [[b]].

9. Use the function composition operator `.` together with any other functions you like, to build a function which, given a list, returns the reverse-sorted list of all its members which are divisible by fifteen.

So Far

1 Numbers ... -3 -2 -1 0 1 2 3... Booleans True and False. Characters like 'X' and '!'.

Mathematical operators + - * which take two numbers and give another.

Operators == < <= > >= /= which compare two values and evaluate to either True or False.

The "conditional" construct **if** *expression1* **then** *expression2* **else** *expression3*, where *expression1* evaluates to something boolean and *expression2* and *expression3* evaluate to the same sort of thing as one another.

The boolean operators && and || which allow us to build compound boolean expressions. The remainder operator `rem`.

2 Assigning a name to an expression using the *name = expression* construct. Building compound expressions using **let** *name1 = expression1* **in let** *name2 = expression2* **in** ...

Functions, introduced by *name argument1 argument2 ... = expression*. These have type $a \rightarrow b$, $a \rightarrow b \rightarrow c$ etc. for some types a, b, c etc. Recursive functions. Turning a two-argument function into an operator with backticks like `rem`.

The types **Bool** and **Char**. The typeclasses **Num**, **Ord**, and **Eq**. A function from values of type a to type b with a in typeclass **Eq** and b in typeclass **Ord** would have type (**Eq** a, **Ord** b) $\Rightarrow$ a $\rightarrow$ b.

The special value it. The command :type and the use of Ctrl-C to interrupt a computation.

3 Matching patterns using f *pattern1 = expression1* ↩ f *pattern2 = expression2* etc... The expressions *expression1, expression2* etc. must have the same type as one another. Writing functions using guarded equations like f x | *guard = expression* ↩ | *guard2 = expression2* | **otherwise** ... The typeclass **Integral**.

4 Lists, which are ordered collections of zero or more elements of like type. They are written between square brackets, with elements separated by commas e.g. [1, 2, 3, 4, 5]. If a list is non-empty, it has a head, which is its first element, and a tail, which is the list composed of the rest of the elements.

The : "cons" operator, which adds an element to the front of a list. The ++ "append" operator, which concatenates two lists together.

Using the : "cons" symbol for pattern matching to distinguish lists of length zero, one, etc. and their contents.

The shorthand list syntax [1 .. 10] and [1, 3 .. 10]. The typeclass **Enum**. List comprehensions [*expression* | name ← *list*, name2 ← *list2*, *guard*, *guard2*].

Strings, which are sequences of characters written between double quotes and are of type [**Char**] or **String**.

5 The `div` operator. The use of **where** as an alternative to **let**.

6 Anonymous functions *name -> expression*. Making operators into functions as in (<) and (+). The . function composition operator. Defining new operators.

Chapter 7

When Things Go Wrong

Some of the functions we have written so far have had a single, correct answer for each possible argument. For example, there is no number we cannot add one to. However, when we use more complicated types such as lists, there are plenty of functions which do not always have an answer – a list might not have a head or a tail, for example. Our take' and drop' functions are unsatisfactory in case of invalid arguments. For example, take' 3 [1] does not complete:

GHCi:

```
Prelude> take' 3 [1]
*** Exception: Non-exhaustive patterns in function take'
```

Haskell provides facilities for dealing with such problems through the **Maybe** type. Something of type **Maybe** a can hold Nothing:

```
x :: Maybe a

x = Nothing
```

Or, it can hold just something of type a

```
y :: Maybe Char

y = Just 'x'
```

Of course, type a can be anything we want. There it was **Char**, making the full type of y **Maybe Char**, here it is **Num** a ⇒ [a], making the full type **Num** a ⇒ **Maybe** [a]:

```
z :: Num a ⇒ Maybe [a]

z = Just [1, 2]
```

of this type anywhere any other type can be used. For example, here is a list of type

```
Just True, Nothing, Nothing, Just False]
```

an now define functions to get the head and tail of a list which use the **Maybe** type to return a useful swer in all cases. If we properly handle every possible case in all our functions, we can be sure that all inputs to our whole program are being dealt with.

```
safeHead :: [a] → Maybe a
safeTail :: [a] → Maybe [a]

safeHead [] = Nothing
safeHead (x:_) = Just x

safeTail [] = Nothing
safeTail (_:xs) = Just xs
```

In the same fashion we can define a function which avoids the division-by-zero error which occurs when the second argument of div is zero, by simply returning Nothing:

```
safeDiv :: Integral a ⇒ a → a → Maybe a

safeDiv _ 0 = Nothing
safeDiv x y = Just (x `div` y)
```

Our take' and drop' functions should never be used with bad inputs – for example trying to take the first three items of a list of length two. However, assuming that the programmer using our head and tail function (it may not be us!) can remember this constraint is unwarranted. By returning something of type **Maybe** [a] we obligate them to do so.

```
safeTake :: (Num a, Ord a) ⇒ a → [b] → Maybe [b]
safeDrop :: (Num a, Ord a) ⇒ a → [b] → Maybe [b]

safeTake n l =
  if n >= 0 && n <= length' l
    then Just (take' n l)
    else Nothing

safeDrop n l =
  if n >= 0 && n <= length' l
    then Just (drop' n l)
    else Nothing
```

We can write a version of our `map'` function provides for the possibility that the mapping may yield `Nothing` for some of its elements. The following function, when given a function of type a → **Maybe** b and a list of type [a] produces a list of type [b] of all the outputs of the function which did not yield `Nothing`:

```
mapMaybe :: (a → Maybe b) → [a] → [b]

mapMaybe _ [] = []
mapMaybe f (x:xs) =
  case f x of
    Nothing -> mapMaybe f xs
    Just r -> r : mapMaybe f xs
```

The **case** ... **of** ... construct allows us to pattern match in the middle of an expression. Let us use `mapMaybe` to find the first elements of a each list in a list of lists, even when some of the lists are empty:

```
GHCi:
Prelude> mapMaybe safeHead [[1, 2, 3], [], [4, 5, 6], []]
[1,4]
```

We can use the **where** construct to avoid writing `mapMaybe f t` twice:

```
mapMaybe :: (a → Maybe b) → [a] → [b]

mapMaybe _ [] = []
mapMaybe f (x:xs) =
  case f x of
    Nothing -> rs
    Just r -> r : rs
  where
    rs = mapMaybe f xs
```

If we wish to carry information about the failure which led to no result being produce for a given input, we can use the **Either** type instead of the **Maybe** type. There are two sorts of thing of type **Either**: `Left` and `Right`. Typically we use `Left` for the results of errors, and `Right` for successful results. For example:

```
GHCi:
Prelude> x = [Right 5, Left "Division by Zero", Right 2]
Prelude> :type x
x :: Num a => [Either [Char] a]
```

Here, the type of `Left` elements is **String**, and the type of `Right` elements is **Num** a ⇒ a. Such an output might be produced by using `map'` and a modified `safeDiv` function:

```
safeDiv :: Integral a ⇒ a → a → Either String a

safeDiv _ 0 = Left "Division by Zero"
safeDiv x y = Right (x `div` y)
```

We can imagine function which return several different messages as Left values. Or, of course, other values which are not strings.

Questions

1. Write a function `smallest` which returns the smallest positive element of a list of numbers. If there is no positive element, it should return `Nothing`.

2. Write another function `smallest0` which uses the `smallest` function but if there is no positive element, returns zero. You might use the **case** ... **of** ... construct here.

3. Write a function `sqrtMaybe` which calculates the largest integer smaller than or equal to the square root of a given number. If the argument is negative, return `Nothing`.

4. Write a version of the `mapMaybe` function which takes a default value, to substitute when `Nothing` is found. Thus, the output list will be the same length as the input list.

5. Write a function `splitEither` which, given a function of type a → **Either** b c and an input list, returns a pair of type (b, c): the first element consisting of all the `Left` results, the second of all the `Right` results. Again, you might use the **case** ... **of** ... construct.

So Far

1 Numbers ... -3 -2 -1 0 1 2 3... Booleans True and False. Characters like 'X' and '!'.

Mathematical operators + - * which take two numbers and give another.

Operators == < <= > >= /= which compare two values and evaluate to either True or False.

The "conditional" construct **if** *expression1* **then** *expression2* **else** *expression3*, where *expression1* evaluates to something boolean and *expression2* and *expression3* evaluate to the same sort of thing as one another.

The boolean operators && and || which allow us to build compound boolean expressions. The remainder operator `rem`.

2 Assigning a name to an expression using the *name = expression* construct. Building compound expressions using **let** *name1 = expression1* **in let** *name2 = expression2* **in** ...

Functions, introduced by *name argument1 argument2 ... = expression*. These have type $a \to b$, $a \to b \to c$ etc. for some types a, b, c etc. Recursive functions. Turning a two-argument function into an operator with backticks like `rem`.

The types **Bool** and **Char**. The typeclasses **Num**, **Ord**, and **Eq**. A function from values of type a to type b with a in typeclass **Eq** and b in typeclass **Ord** would have type (**Eq** a, **Ord** b) $\Rightarrow$ a $\to$ b.

The special value it. The command :type and the use of Ctrl-C to interrupt a computation.

3 Matching patterns using f *pattern1 = expression1* ↩ f *pattern2 = expression2* etc... The expressions *expression1, expression2* etc. must have the same type as one another. Writing functions using guarded equations like f x | *guard = expression* ↩ | *guard2 = expression2* | **otherwise** ... The typeclass **Integral**.

4 Lists, which are ordered collections of zero or more elements of like type. They are written between square brackets, with elements separated by commas e.g. [1, 2, 3, 4, 5]. If a list is non-empty, it has a head, which is its first element, and a tail, which is the list composed of the rest of the elements.

The : "cons" operator, which adds an element to the front of a list. The ++ "append" operator, which concatenates two lists together.

Using the : "cons" symbol for pattern matching to distinguish lists of length zero, one, etc. and their contents.

The shorthand list syntax [1 .. 10] and [1, 3 .. 10]. The typeclass **Enum**. List comprehensions [*expression* | name ← *list*, name2 ← *list2*, *guard*, *guard2*].

Strings, which are sequences of characters written between double quotes and are of type [**Char**] or **String**.

5 The `div` operator. The use of **where** as an alternative to **let**.

6 Anonymous functions *name -> expression*. Making operators into functions as in (<) and (+). The . function composition operator. Defining new operators.

7 The **Maybe** type with its constructors Nothing and Just. The **Either** type with its constructors Left and Right. The **case** ... **of** ... construct.

Chapter 8

Looking Things Up

Many programs make use of a structure known as a *dictionary*. A real dictionary is used for associating definitions with words; we use "dictionary" more generally to mean associating some unique *keys* (like words) with *values* (like definitions). For example, we might like to store the following information about the number of people living in each house in a road:

House	People
1	4
2	2
3	2
4	3
5	1
6	2

The house number is the key, the number of people living in the house is the value. The order of keys is unimportant – we just need to be able to associate each key with one (and only one) value. It would be very inconvenient to store two lists, one of house numbers and one of people. For one thing, we would have no way of guaranteeing the two lists were of equal length. What we would like is a way of representing pairs like (1, 4) and then having a single list of those. To make a pair in Haskell, just write it with parentheses and a comma:

```
p :: (Num a, Num b) ⇒ (a, b)

p = (1, 4)
```

Its type is written likewise. Note that the two parts of the pair need not be of the same type, which is why we do not see **Num** a ⇒ (a, a). Here is another example:

```
q :: Num a ⇒ (a, Char)

q = (1, '1')
```

We can write simple functions to extract the first and second element using pattern matching:

```
fst' :: (a, b) → a
snd' :: (a, b) → b

fst' (x, _) = x
snd' (_, y) = y
```

Using pairs, we can store a dictionary as a list of pairs:

```
census :: (Num a, Num b) ⇒ [(a, b)]

census = [(1, 4), (2, 2), (3, 2), (4, 3), (5, 1), (6, 2)]
```

What operations might we want on dictionaries? We certainly need to look up a value given a key:

```
lookup' :: Eq a ⇒ a → [(a, b)] → Maybe b

lookup' k' [] = Nothing                     we reached the end, and did not find it
lookup' k' ((k, v):xs) =
  if k == k' then Just v else lookup' k' xs      return value, or keep looking
```

For example, lookup' 4 census evaluates to Just 3, whereas lookup' 9 census evaluates to Nothing. Another basic operation is to add an entry. We must replace it if the key already exists, to maintain the property that each key appears at most once in a dictionary:

```
add :: Eq a ⇒ a → b → [(a, b)] → [(a, b)]

add k v [] = [(k, v)]                            it is not present, so add it
add k v ((k', v'):xs) =
    if k == k'
      then (k, v) : xs           found an equal key so replace the entry
      else (k', v') : add k v xs    otherwise, keep the entry and continue
```

For example, add 6 2 [(4, 5), (6, 3)] evaluates to [(4, 5), (6, 2)] (the value for key 6 is replaced), whereas add 6 2 [(4, 5), (3, 6)] evaluates to [(4, 5), (3, 6), (6, 2)] (the new entry for key 6 is added). Removing an element is easy:

```
remove :: Eq a ⇒ a → [(a, b)] → [(a, b)]

remove k [] = []                                     it is not present, so we are done
remove k ((k', v'):xs) =
  if k == k'
    then xs                              equal key – remove it, and we are done
    else (k', v') : remove k xs              otherwise, retain and keep looking
```

The function always succeeds – even if the key was not found. We can use our lookup' operation to build a function which checks if a key exists within a dictionary:

```
keyExists :: (Eq a, Eq b) ⇒ a → [(a, b)] → Bool

keyExists k d =
  lookup' k d /= Nothing
```

Pairs are just a particular instance of a more general construct – the *tuple*. A tuple may contain two or more things. For example, ('b', False, 'a') has type (**Char**, **Bool**, **Char**).

Questions

1. Write a function to determine the number of different keys in a dictionary.

2. Define a function `replace` which is like `add`, but returns `Nothing` if the key is already present.

3. Write a function to build a dictionary from two lists, one containing keys and another containing values. If the lists are not of equal length, return `Nothing`. You may assume there are no duplicate keys.

4. Now write the inverse function: given a dictionary, return the pair of two lists – the first containing all the keys, and the second containing all the values.

5. Define a function to turn any list of pairs into a dictionary. If duplicate keys are found, the value associated with the first occurrence of the key should be kept.

6. Write the function `union a b` which forms the union of two dictionaries. The union of two dictionaries is the dictionary containing all the entries in one or other or both. In the case that a key is contained in both dictionaries, the value in the first should be preferred.

So Far

1 Numbers ...-3 -2 -1 0 1 2 3...Booleans True and False. Characters like 'X' and '!'.

Mathematical operators + - * which take two numbers and give another.

Operators == < <= > >= /= which compare two values and evaluate to either True or False.

The "conditional" construct **if** *expression1* **then** *expression2* **else** *expression3*, where *expression1* evaluates to something boolean and *expression2* and *expression3* evaluate to the same sort of thing as one another.

The boolean operators && and || which allow us to build compound boolean expressions. The remainder operator `rem`.

2 Assigning a name to an expression using the *name = expression* construct. Building compound expressions using **let** *name1 = expression1* **in let** *name2 = expression2* **in** ...

Functions, introduced by *name argument1 argument2 ... = expression*. These have type $a \rightarrow b$, $a \rightarrow b \rightarrow c$ etc. for some types a, b, c etc. Recursive functions. Turning a two-argument function into an operator with backticks like `rem`.

The types **Bool** and **Char**. The typeclasses **Num**, **Ord**, and **Eq**. A function from values of type a to type b with a in typeclass **Eq** and b in typeclass **Ord** would have type (**Eq** a, **Ord** b) $\Rightarrow$ a $\rightarrow$ b.

The special value it. The command :type and the use of Ctrl-C to interrupt a computation.

3 Matching patterns using f *pattern1 = expression1* ↩ f *pattern2 = expression2* etc... The expressions *expression1, expression2* etc. must have the same type as one another. Writing functions using guarded equations like f x | *guard = expression* ↩ | *guard2 = expression2* | **otherwise** ... The typeclass **Integral**.

4 Lists, which are ordered collections of zero or more elements of like type. They are written between square brackets, with elements separated by commas e.g. [1, 2, 3, 4, 5]. If a list is non-empty, it has a head, which is its first element, and a tail, which is the list composed of the rest of the elements.

The : "cons" operator, which adds an element to the front of a list. The ++ "append" operator, which concatenates two lists together.

Using the : "cons" symbol for pattern matching to distinguish lists of length zero, one, etc. and their contents.

The shorthand list syntax [1 .. 10] and [1, 3 .. 10]. The typeclass **Enum**. List comprehensions [*expression* | name ← *list*, name2 ← *list2*, *guard*, *guard2*].

Strings, which are sequences of characters written between double quotes and are of type [**Char**] or **String**.

5 The `div` operator. The use of **where** as an alternative to **let**.

6 Anonymous functions *name* -> *expression*. Making operators into functions as in (<) and (+). The . function composition operator. Defining new operators.

7 The **Maybe** type with its constructors Nothing and Just. The **Either** type with its constructors Left and Right. The **case** ... **of** ... construct.

8 Tuples to combine a fixed number of elements (x, y), (x, y, z) etc. with types (a, b), (a, b, c) etc.

Chapter 9

More with Functions

Look again at the type of a simple function with more than one argument:

```
add :: Num a ⇒ a → a → a

add x y = x + y
```

We have been considering functions like this as taking two arguments and returning a result. In fact, the truth is a little different. The type **Num** a $\Rightarrow$ a $\rightarrow$ a $\rightarrow$ a can also be written as **Num** a $\Rightarrow$ a $\rightarrow$ (a $\rightarrow$ a). Haskell lets us omit the parentheses because $\rightarrow$ is a right-associative operator in the language of types. This gives us a clue.

> *In truth, the function **add** is a function which, when you give it a number, gives you a function which, when you give it an number, gives the sum.*

This would be of no particular interest to us, except for one thing: we can give a function with two arguments just one argument at a time, and it turns out to be rather useful. For example:

```
GHCi:
Prelude> add x y = x + y
Prelude> :type add
add :: Num a => a -> a -> a
Prelude> f = add 6
Prelude> :type f
f :: Num a => a -> a
Prelude> f 5
11
```

Here, we have defined a function f by applying just one argument to add. This gives a function of type **Num** a $\Rightarrow$ a $\rightarrow$ a which adds 6 to any number. We then apply 5 to this function, giving 11. When defining f, we used *partial application* (we applied only some of the arguments). In fact, even when applying all the arguments at once, we could equally write (add 6) 5 rather than add 6 5. We can add six to every element in a list:

GHCi:
Prelude> map' (add 6) [10, 20, 30]
[16,26,36]

Here, add 6 has the type **Num** a $\Rightarrow$ a $\rightarrow$ a, which is an appropriate type to be the first argument to map' when mapping over a list of numbers. Recall the function to map something over a list of lists from the questions to Chapter 6:

```
mapl :: (a → b) → [[a]] → [[b]]

mapl f [] = []
mapl f (x:xs) = map' f x : mapl f xs
```

With partial application, we can write

```
mapl :: (a → b) → [[a]] → [[b]]

mapl f l = map' (map' f) l
```

Can you see why? The partially applied function map' f is of type a $\rightarrow$ b, which is exactly the right type to pass to map' when mapping over lists of lists. In fact, we can go even further and write:

```
mapl :: (a → b) → [[a]] → [[b]]

mapl f = map' (map' f)
```

Here, map' (map' f) has type [[a]] $\rightarrow$ [[b]] so when an f is supplied to mapl, a function is returned requiring just the list. This is partial application at work again. We can use the . operator from Chapter 6 to simplify further:

```
mapl :: (a → b) → [[a]] → [[b]]

mapl = map' . map'
```

You can see the real structure of multiple-argument functions, by writing add using anonymous functions:

```
add :: Num a ⇒ a → a → a

add = \x -> \y -> x + y
```

This makes it more obvious that our two-argument add function is really just composed of one-argument functions, but add x y = x + y is much clearer. We can apply one or more arguments at a time, but they must be applied in order. Everything in this chapter also works for functions with more than two arguments.

Haskell includes a nicer way to write partially-applied functions based on operators. These are called *operator sections*. We may write (/ 2) for the function which divides anything by two, or (20 /) for the function which divides twenty by anything, for example. The section (1 :) adds 1 at the beginning of any list of numbers. Here, we use an operator section to divide every number in a list by two:

```
GHCi:
Prelude> map' (/ 2) [10, 20, 30]
[5,10,15]
```

SUMMARY

The function f x y has type a → b → c which can also be written a → (b → c). Thus, it takes an argument of type a and returns a function of type b → c which, when you give it an argument of type b returns something of type c. And so, we can apply just one argument to the function f (which is called partial application), or apply both at once. When we write f x y = . . . this is just shorthand for f = \x -> \y ->
. . .

Questions

1. Rewrite the summary paragraph at the end of this chapter for the three argument function `g a b c`.

2. Recall the function `elem' e l` which determines if an element `e` is contained in a list `l`. What is its type? What is the type of `elem' e`? Use partial application to write a function `elemAll e ls` which determines if an element is a member of all the lists in the list of lists `ls`.

3. Write a function `mapll` which maps a function over lists of lists of lists, using the technique described in this chapter.

4. Write a function `truncateList` which takes an integer and a list of lists, and returns a list of lists, each of which has been truncated to the given length. If a list is shorter than the given length, it is unchanged. Make use of partial application.

5. Write a function which takes a list of lists of numbers and returns the list composed of all the first elements of the lists. If a list is empty, a given number should be used in place of its first element.

6. Use an operator section to write a function which puts a given number onto the front of all the lists in a list of lists of numbers.

So Far

1 Numbers ...`-3 -2 -1 0 1 2 3`...Booleans `True` and `False`. Characters like `'X'` and `'!'`.

Mathematical operators `+ - *` which take two numbers and give another.

Operators `== < <= > >= /=` which compare two values and evaluate to either `True` or `False`.

The "conditional" construct **if** *expression1* **then** *expression2* **else** *expression3*, where *expression1* evaluates to something boolean and *expression2* and *expression3* evaluate to the same sort of thing as one another.

The boolean operators `&&` and `||` which allow us to build compound boolean expressions. The remainder operator `` `rem` ``.

2 Assigning a name to an expression using the *name = expression* construct. Building compound expressions using **let** *name1 = expression1* **in let** *name2 = expression2* **in** ...

Functions, introduced by *name argument1 argument2 ... = expression*. These have type $a \rightarrow b$, $a \rightarrow b \rightarrow c$ etc. for some types a, b, c etc. Recursive functions. Turning a two-argument function into an operator with backticks like `` `rem` ``.

The types **Bool** and **Char**. The typeclasses **Num**, **Ord**, and **Eq**. A function from values of type a to type b with a in typeclass **Eq** and b in typeclass **Ord** would have type (**Eq** a, **Ord** b) $\Rightarrow$ a $\rightarrow$ b.

The special value `it`. The command `:type` and the use of Ctrl-C to interrupt a computation.

3 Matching patterns using f *pattern1 = expression1* ↩ f *pattern2 = expression2* etc... The expressions *expression1, expression2* etc. must have the same type as one another. Writing functions using guarded equations like f x | *guard = expression* ↩ | *guard2 = expression2* | **otherwise** ... The typeclass **Integral**.

4 Lists, which are ordered collections of zero or more elements of like type. They are written between square brackets, with elements separated by commas e.g. `[1, 2, 3, 4, 5]`. If a list is non-empty, it has a head, which is its first element, and a tail, which is the list composed of the rest of the elements.

The `:` "cons" operator, which adds an element to the front of a list. The `++` "append" operator, which concatenates two lists together.

Using the `:` "cons" symbol for pattern matching to distinguish lists of length zero, one, etc. and their contents.

The shorthand list syntax `[1 .. 10]` and `[1, 3 .. 10]`. The typeclass **Enum**. List comprehensions [*expression* | *name* ← *list, name2* ← *list2, guard, guard2*].

Strings, which are sequences of characters written between double quotes and are of type [**Char**] or **String**.

5 The `` `div` `` operator. The use of **where** as an alternative to **let**.

6 Anonymous functions *name -> expression*. Making operators into functions as in (`<`) and (`+`). The `.` function composition operator. Defining new operators.

7 The **Maybe** type with its constructors `Nothing` and `Just`. The **Either** type with its constructors `Left` and `Right`. The **case** ... **of** ... construct.

8 Tuples to combine a fixed number of elements (x, y), (x, y, z) etc. with types (a, b), (a, b, c) etc.

9 Partial application of functions by giving fewer than the full number of arguments. Operator sections like (`10 /`).

Chapter 10

New Kinds of Data

So far, we have considered types for numbers, and others like **Bool** and **Char**. We have seen the compound types of lists and tuples. We have built functions from and to these types. It would be possible to encode anything we wanted as lists and tuples of these types, but it would lead to complex and error-strewn programs. It is time to make our own types. New types are introduced using **data**. Here is a type for colours:

```
GHCi:
Prelude> data Colour = Red | Green | Blue | Yellow
Prelude> :type Red
Red :: Colour
```

The name of our new type is Colour (it must have a capital letter). It has four *constructors*, written with initial capital letters: Red, Green, Blue, and Yellow. These are the possible forms a value of type colour may take. Now we can build values of type Colour:

```
col :: Colour
cols :: [Colour]
colpair :: (Char, Colour)

col = Blue

cols = [Red, Red, Green, Yellow]

colpair = ('R', Red)
```

We notice an immediate problem, though. Haskell does not seem to know how to print out the values of our new type:

```
GHCi:
Prelude> data Colour = Red | Green | Blue | Yellow
Prelude> col = Blue
```

```
Prelude> col

<interactive>:4:1: error:
    • No instance for (Show Colour) arising from a use of 'print'
    • In a stmt of an interactive GHCi command: print it
```

If we are happy for Haskell to try to work out automatically how to print values of type Colour we can use write **deriving** Show after the type:

```
Prelude> data Colour = Red | Green | Blue | Yellow deriving Show
Prelude> col = Blue
Prelude> col
Blue
```

The word **deriving** tells Haskell to try to work out automatically (to derive) how to make Colour an instance of the type class **Show**, which is the class of all types which can be automatically printed out. Most of the types we have seen so far (booleans, numbers, lists, tuples, but not functions) are instances of the typeclass **Show**, which is why Haskell can print them. The reason we do not see, for example (**Num** a, **Show** a) ⇒ a for a number is that, since **Num** is a *subclass* of **Show**, we need only write **Num**, and **Show** is implied. Now that we have used **deriving**, Colour is also an instance of **Show**. In fact, the built-in function to show any showable thing, which Haskell uses, is called show and we can use it ourselves:

```
GHCi:
Prelude> show [1, 2, 3]
"[1,2,3]"
```

What is the type of the built-in show function? It is **Show** a ⇒ a → **String** because, given anything which is showable, it produces a **String** representing it.

Type definitions may contain a *type variable* like a to allow the type of part of the new type to vary – i.e. for the type to be polymorphic. For example, we can define the **Maybe** type ourselves.

```
data Maybe a = Nothing | Just a deriving Show
```

In addition to being polymorphic, new types may also be recursively defined. We can use this functionality to define our own lists, just like the built-in lists in Haskell but without the special notation:

```
data Sequence a = Nil | Cons a (Sequence a) deriving Show
```

We have called our type Sequence to avoid confusion. It has two constructors: Nil which is equivalent to [], and Cons which is equivalent to the : operator. Cons carries two pieces of data with it – one of type a (the head) and one of type Sequence a (the tail). This is the recursive part of our definition. Now we can make our own lists equivalent to Haskell's built-in ones:

Built-in	Ours	Our Type
[]	Nil	Sequence a
['a', 'x', 'e']	Cons 'a' (Cons 'x' (Cons 'e' Nil)))	Sequence **Char**
[1]	Cons 1 Nil	**Num** a ⇒ Sequence a
[Red, RGB 2 2 2]	Cons (Red, Cons (RGB (2, 2, 2), Nil))	**Num** a ⇒ Sequence (Colour a)

Now you can see why getting at the last element of a list in Haskell is harder than getting at the first element – it is deeper in the structure. Let us compare some functions on Haskell lists with the same ones on our new Sequence type. First, the ones for built-in lists.

```
length' :: Num b ⇒ [a] → b
append :: [a] → [a] → [a]

length' [] = 0
length' (_:xs) = 1 + length' xs

append [] ys = ys
append (x:xs) ys = x : append xs ys
```

And now the same functions with our new Sequence type:

```
seqLength :: Num b ⇒ Sequence a → b
seqAppend :: Sequence a → Sequence a → Sequence a

seqLength Nil = 0
seqLength (Cons _ xs) = 1 + seqLength xs

seqAppend Nil ys = ys
seqAppend (Cons x xs) ys = Cons x (seqAppend xs ys)
```

Notice how all the conveniences of pattern matching such as the use of the underscore work for our own types too.

A Type for Mathematical Expressions

Our Sequence was an example of a recursively-defined type, which can be processed naturally by recursive functions. Mathematical expressions can be modeled in the same way. For example, the expression $1 + 2 \times 3$ could be drawn like this:

Notice that, in this representation, we never need parentheses – the diagram is unambiguous. We can evaluate the expression by reducing each part in turn:

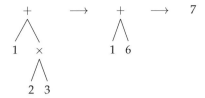

Here is a suitable type for such expressions:

```
data Expr a = Num a
            | Add (Expr a) (Expr a)
            | Subtract (Expr a) (Expr a)
            | Multiply (Expr a) (Expr a)
            | Divide (Expr a) (Expr a) deriving Show
```

For example, the expression $1 + 2 * 3$ is represented in this data type as:

```
Add (Num 1) (Multiply (Num 2) (Num 3))
```

We can now write a function to evaluate expressions:

```
evaluate :: Integral a ⇒ Expr a → a

evaluate (Num x) = x
evaluate (Add e e') = evaluate e + evaluate e'
evaluate (Subtract e e') = evaluate e - evaluate e'
evaluate (Multiply e e') = evaluate e * evaluate e'
evaluate (Divide e e') = evaluate e `div` evaluate e'
```

Building our own types leads to clearer programs with more predictable behaviour, and helps us to think about a problem – often the functions are easy to write once we have decided on appropriate types.

Questions

1. Design a new type Rect a for representing rectangles. Treat squares as a special case.

2. Now write a function of type **Num** a $\Rightarrow$ Rect a $\rightarrow$ a to calculate the area of a given Rect.

3. Write a function which rotates a Rect such that it is at least as tall as it is wide.

4. Use this function to write one which, given a [Rect], returns another such list which has the smallest total width and whose members are sorted narrowest first.

5. Write versions of the `seqTake`, `seqDrop`, and `seqMap` functions for the Sequence type.

6. Extend the Expr type and the `evaluate` function to allow raising a number to a power.

7. Use the **Maybe** type to deal with the problem that a division by zero may occur in the `evaluate` function.

So Far

1 Numbers ... -3 -2 -1 0 1 2 3... Booleans True and False. Characters like 'X' and '!'.

Mathematical operators + - * which take two numbers and give another.

Operators == < <= > >= /= which compare two values and evaluate to either True or False.

The "conditional" construct **if** *expression1* **then** *expression2* **else** *expression3*, where *expression1* evaluates to something boolean and *expression2* and *expression3* evaluate to the same sort of thing as one another.

The boolean operators && and || which allow us to build compound boolean expressions. The remainder operator `rem`.

2 Assigning a name to an expression using the *name = expression* construct. Building compound expressions using **let** *name1 = expression1* **in let** *name2 = expression2* **in** ...

Functions, introduced by *name argument1 argument2 ... = expression*. These have type $a \rightarrow b$, $a \rightarrow b \rightarrow c$ etc. for some types a, b, c etc. Recursive functions. Turning a two-argument function into an operator with backticks like `rem`.

The types **Bool** and **Char**. The typeclasses **Num, Ord,** and **Eq**. A function from values of type a to type b with a in typeclass **Eq** and b in typeclass **Ord** would have type (**Eq** a, **Ord** b) $\Rightarrow$ a $\rightarrow$ b.

The special value it. The command :type and the use of Ctrl-C to interrupt a computation.

3 Matching patterns using f *pattern1 = expression1* ↩ f *pattern2 = expression2* etc... The expressions *expression1, expression2* etc. must have the same type as one another. Writing functions using guarded equations like f x | *guard = expression* ↩ | *guard2 = expression2* | **otherwise** ... The typeclass **Integral**.

4 Lists, which are ordered collections of zero or more elements of like type. They are written between square brackets, with elements separated by commas e.g. [1, 2, 3, 4, 5]. If a list is non-empty, it has a head, which is its first element, and a tail, which is the list composed of the rest of the elements.

The : "cons" operator, which adds an element to the front of a list. The ++ "append" operator, which concatenates two lists together.

Using the : "cons" symbol for pattern matching to distinguish lists of length zero, one, etc. and their contents.

The shorthand list syntax [1 .. 10] and [1, 3 .. 10]. The typeclass **Enum**. List comprehensions [*expression | name ← list, name2 ← list2, guard, guard2*].

Strings, which are sequences of characters written between double quotes and are of type [**Char**] or **String**.

5 The `div` operator. The use of **where** as an alternative to **let**.

6 Anonymous functions *name -> expression*. Making operators into functions as in (<) and (+). The . function composition operator. Defining new operators.

7 The **Maybe** type with its constructors Nothing and Just. The **Either** type with its constructors Left and Right. The **case** ... **of** ... construct.

8 Tuples to combine a fixed number of elements (x, y), (x, y, z) etc. with types (a, b), (a, b, c) etc.

9 Partial application of functions by giving fewer than the full number of arguments. Operator sections like (10 /).

10 New types with **data**. The **Show** typeclass. Implementing **Show** automatically with **deriving**. The show function to create strings from things of other types.

Chapter 11

Growing Trees

We have used lists to represent collections of elements of like type but varying length, and tuples to represent collections of things of any type but fixed length. Another common data type is the *binary tree*, which is used to represent structures which branch, such as the arithmetical expressions we constructed in the last chapter.

How can we represent such trees using a Haskell type? When we built our version of the Haskell list type, we had two constructors – Cons to hold a head and a tail, and Nil to represent the end of the list. With a tree, we need a version of Cons which can hold two tails – the left and right, and we still need a version of Nil.

```
data Tree a = Br a (Tree a) (Tree a)                    branch
            | Lf deriving Show                            leaf
```

Our type is called Tree, and is polymorphic (can hold any sort of data at the branches). There are two constructors: Br for branches, which hold three things: an element (of type a), the left sub-tree (of type Tree a), and the right sub-tree (of type Tree a). If it is not a Br, it is a Lf (leaf), which is used to signal that there is no left, or no right sub-tree. Here are some examples of trees expressed as values of our new type:

1   is written as   Br 1 Lf Lf

2   is written as   Br 2 (Br 1 Lf Lf) Lf

1

 2   is written as   Br 2 (Br 1 Lf Lf) (Br 4 Lf Lf)

The empty tree is simply Lf. You can see now why we used abbreviated constructor names – even small trees result in long textual representations. Let us write some simple functions on trees. To calculate the number of elements in the tree, we just count one for each branch, and zero for each leaf:

```
treeSize :: Num b ⇒ Tree a → b

treeSize (Br _ l r) = 1 + treeSize l + treeSize r
treeSize Lf = 0
```

Notice that the recursive function follows the shape of the recursive type. A similar function can be used to add up all the integers in a tree of numbers:

```
treeTotal :: Num a ⇒ Tree a → a

treeTotal (Br x l r) = x + treeTotal l + treeTotal r
treeTotal Lf = 0
```

How can we calculate the maximum depth of a tree? The depth is the longest path from the root (top) of the tree to a leaf.

```
max' :: Ord a ⇒ a → a → a
maxDepth :: (Num b, Ord b) ⇒ Tree a → b

max' a b = if a > b then a else b

maxDepth (Br _ l r) = 1 + max' (maxDepth l) (maxDepth r)
maxDepth Lf = 0
```

We defined a function max' which returns the larger of two integers. Then, in our main function, we count a leaf as zero depth, and calculate the depth of a branch as one plus the maximum of the left and right sub-trees coming from that branch. Now consider extracting all of the elements from a tree into a list:

```
listOfTree :: Tree a → [a]

listOfTree (Br x l r) = listOfTree l ++ [x] ++ listOfTree r
listOfTree Lf = []
```

Notice that we chose to put all the elements on the left branch before the current element, and all the elements in the right branch after. This is arbitrary – it is clear that there are multiple answers to the question "How can I extract all the elements from a tree as a list?". Before we consider real applications of trees, let us look at one more function. Here is how to map over trees:

```
treeMap :: (a → b) → Tree a → Tree b

treeMap f (Br x l r) = Br (f x) (treeMap f l) (treeMap f r)
treeMap f Lf = Lf
```

Notice the similarity to our `map'` function for lists, both in the type and the definition.

Using trees to build better dictionaries

We have seen that arithmetic expressions can be drawn as trees on paper, and we have designed a Haskell data type for binary trees to hold any sort of element. Now it is time to introduce the most important application of trees: the *binary search tree*, which is another way of implementing the dictionary *data structure* we described in Chapter 8.

The most important advantage of a tree is that it is often very much easier to reach a given element. When searching in a dictionary defined as a list, it took on average time proportional to the number of items in the dictionary to find a value for a key (the position of the required entry is, on average, halfway along the list). If we use a binary tree, and if it is reasonably nicely balanced in shape, that time can be reduced to the logarithm base two of the number of elements in the dictionary. Can you see why?

We can use our existing Tree type. In the case of a dictionary, it will have type Tree (a, b), in other words a tree of key-value pairs where the keys have some type a and the values some type b. So, our tree representing a dictionary mapping integers like 1 to their spellings like "one" would have type **Num** a ⇒ Tree (a, **String**):

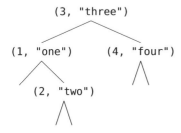

This would be written in Haskell like so:

```
Br (3, "three") (Br (1, "one") Lf (Br (2, "two") Lf Lf)) (Br (4, "four") Lf Lf)
```

If we arrange the tree such that, at each branch, everything to the left has a key less than the key at the branch, and everything to the right has a key greater than that at the branch, we have a *binary search tree*.

Lookup is simple: start at the top, and if we have not found the key we are looking for, go left or right depending upon whether the required key is smaller or larger than the value at the current branch. If we reach a leaf, the key was not in the tree.

```
treeLookup :: Ord a ⇒ Tree (a, b) → a → Maybe b

treeLookup Lf _ = Nothing
treeLookup (Br (k', v) l r) k =
  if k == k' then Just v else                          found the key – return the value
  if k < k' then treeLookup l k else                                          go left
    treeLookup r k                                                           go right
```

How can we insert a new key-value pair into an existing tree? We can find the position to insert by using the same procedure as the lookup function – going left or right at each branch as appropriate. If we find an equal key, we put our new value there instead. Otherwise, we will end up at a leaf, and this is the insertion point – thus, if the key is not in the dictionary when `treeInsert` is used, it will be added in place of an existing leaf.

```
treeInsert :: Ord a ⇒ Tree (a, b) → a → b → Tree (a, b)

treeInsert Lf k v = Br (k, v) Lf Lf                                      insert at leaf
treeInsert (Br (k', v') l r) k v =
  if k == k' then Br (k, v) l r else                                    replace value
  if k < k' then Br (k', v') (treeInsert l k v) r else                       go left
    Br (k', v') l (treeInsert r k v)                                         go right
```

For example, if we wish to insert the value `"zero"` for the key 0 in the tree drawn above, we would obtain

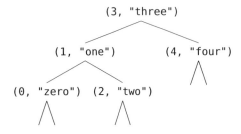

The shape of the tree is dependent upon the order of insertions into the tree – if they are in order (or reverse order), we obtain a rather inefficient tree – no better a dictionary than a list in fact. However, on average, we obtain a reasonably balanced tree, and logarithmic lookup and insertion times.

Lists and trees are examples of *data structures*. The design of an algorithm and its data structures are intimately connected.

Questions

1. Write a function of type **Eq** a $\Rightarrow$ a $\rightarrow$ Tree a $\rightarrow$ **Bool** to determine if a given element is in a tree.

2. Write a function which flips a tree left to right such that, if it were drawn on paper, it would appear to be a mirror image.

3. Write a function to determine if two trees have the same shape, irrespective of the actual values of the elements.

4. Write a function `treeOfList` which builds a tree representation of a dictionary from a list representation of a dictionary.

5. Write a function to combine two dictionaries represented as trees into one. In the case of clashing keys, prefer the value from the first dictionary.

6. Can you define a type for trees which, instead of branching exactly two ways each time, can branch zero or more ways, possibly different at each branch? Write simple functions like our `treeSize`, `treeTotal`, and `treeMap` for your new type of tree.

So Far

1 Numbers ...-3 -2 -1 0 1 2 3...Booleans True and False. Characters like 'X' and '!'.

Mathematical operators + - * which take two numbers and give another.

Operators == < <= > >= /= which compare two values and evaluate to either True or False.

The "conditional" construct **if** *expression1* **then** *expression2* **else** *expression3*, where *expression1* evaluates to something boolean and *expression2* and *expression3* evaluate to the same sort of thing as one another.

The boolean operators && and || which allow us to build compound boolean expressions. The remainder operator `rem`.

2 Assigning a name to an expression using the *name = expression* construct. Building compound expressions using **let** *name1 = expression1* **in let** *name2 = expression2* **in** ...

Functions, introduced by *name argument1 argument2 ... = expression*. These have type $a \rightarrow b$, $a \rightarrow b \rightarrow c$ etc. for some types a, b, c etc. Recursive functions. Turning a two-argument function into an operator with backticks like `rem`.

The types **Bool** and **Char**. The typeclasses **Num**, **Ord**, and **Eq**. A function from values of type a to type b with a in typeclass **Eq** and b in typeclass **Ord** would have type (**Eq** a, **Ord** b) $\Rightarrow$ a $\rightarrow$ b.

The special value it. The command :type and the use of Ctrl-C to interrupt a computation.

3 Matching patterns using f *pattern1 = expression1* ↩ f *pattern2 = expression2* etc... The expressions *expression1, expression2* etc. must have the same type as one another. Writing functions using guarded equations like f x | *guard = expression* ↩ | *guard2 = expression2* | **otherwise** ... The typeclass **Integral**.

4 Lists, which are ordered collections of zero or more elements of like type. They are written between square brackets, with elements separated by commas e.g. [1, 2, 3, 4, 5]. If a list is non-empty, it has a head, which is its first element, and a tail, which is the list composed of the rest of the elements.

The : "cons" operator, which adds an element to the front of a list. The ++ "append" operator, which concatenates two lists together.

Using the : "cons" symbol for pattern matching to distinguish lists of length zero, one, etc. and their contents.

The shorthand list syntax [1 .. 10] and [1, 3 .. 10]. The typeclass **Enum**. List comprehensions [*expression* | *name ← list*, name2 ← *list2, guard, guard2*].

Strings, which are sequences of characters written between double quotes and are of type [**Char**] or **String**.

5 The `div` operator. The use of **where** as an alternative to **let**.

6 Anonymous functions *name -> expression*. Making operators into functions as in (<) and (+). The . function composition operator. Defining new operators.

7 The **Maybe** type with its constructors Nothing and Just. The **Either** type with its constructors Left and Right. The **case** ... **of** ... construct.

8 Tuples to combine a fixed number of elements (x, y), (x, y, z) etc. with types (a, b), (a, b, c) etc.

9 Partial application of functions by giving fewer than the full number of arguments. Operator sections like (10 /).

10 New types with **data**. The **Show** typeclass. Implementing **Show** automatically with **deriving**. The show function to create strings from things of other types.

Chapter 12

The Other Numbers

Most of our numbers thus far have been of the somewhat mercurial **Num** a $\Rightarrow$ a type. In Chapter 3 we met the **Integral** typeclass. It is time, at last, to meet the rest of the family, and to explain this complexity. Why is Haskell's system of numbers so seemingly complicated? Historically, many serious errors in computer programs have arisen from programmers mixing mathematically different sorts of number, and processing them with functions intended for other sorts. Haskell uses a more rigorous separation and categorisation of the different sorts of number to help us avoid such mistakes. The price, in terms of learning about the different number typeclasses, is worth paying – especially as we build larger and more complex programs.

All types which are instances of the **Num** typeclass provide the operators +, -, and *, which we have already seen, and they operate on all sorts of numbers:

```
GHCi:
Prelude> 2 * 4
8
Prelude> 2.0 * 4.0
8.0
```

Since the text representing a number (such as "4") can play the part of any sort of number, it is fine to write this:

```
GHCi:
Prelude> 2.0 * 4
8.0
Prelude> :type 4
Num a => a
```

Haskell knows how to make sure that 4 is treated as a real number here, because it is multiplied by a real number, and both operands of a * operator must have the same sort of number. It is worth considering one more operator provided by every instance of the typeclass **Num** – that is, unary (of one operand) negation. When we write -4.5 we are writing the literal number 4.5 and negating it with the unary operator -. Unary negation binds less tightly that, for example, multiplication, which leads to the following apparent confusion:

```
GHCi:
Prelude> -4 * 2
-8
Prelude> 4 * -2
```

```
<interactive> error:
    Precedence parsing error
        cannot mix '*' [infixl 7] and prefix '-' [infixl 6]
        in the same infix expression
```

But, in fact, there is no asymmetry here. The expression -4 * 2 means -(4 * 2) since multiplication has the higher precedence. If in doubt, use parentheses, and write, for example (-4) * 2 or 4 * (-2).

The **Num** typeclass does not define the division operator /, since some numbers require functions for integer division and remainder, and some real division. We have already met the typeclass **Integral**, which provides the division-and-remainder operations rem and div on whole numbers. It is a subclass of the typeclass **Num**, meaning that it provides all the operations provided by **Num**, and some more. We can show the relationship like this:

As a reminder, here is our function definition from Chapter 3 which resulted in a type involving the **Integral** typeclass:

```
gcd' :: Integral a ⇒ a → a → a

gcd' a b =
  if b == 0 then a else gcd' b (a `rem` b)
```

What this type tells us is that the function operates on any number type a, so long as that type is an instance of typeclass **Integral**. If a type is only an instance of **Num**, but not of **Integral**, the rem function cannot operate on it, and so neither can gcd', because it uses rem.

When we type a whole number, Haskell gives it type **Num** a ⇒ a. What about when we type a number with a decimal point in it?

```
GHCi:
Prelude> :type 4.0
4.0 :: Fractional a => a
```

Fractional is another subclass of **Num**. This time it provides the real division operator, rather than the division and remainder operators of the **Integral** typeclass:

```
GHCi:
Prelude> 4.0 / 3.7
1.081081081081081
Prelude> :type 4.0 / 3.7
4.0 / 3.7 :: Fractional a => a
```

Now, we can extend our diagram showing the relationship between the typeclasses:

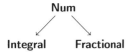

So, when we type a number with a decimal point it must be a **Fractional** a ⇒ a, but when we type one without a decimal point it can act as any instance of **Num**. So we can use the division operator on what look like whole numbers too:

```
GHCi:
Prelude> 4 / 3
1.081081081081081
Prelude> :type 4 / 3
4 / 3 :: Fractional a => a
Prelude> :type ( / )
( / ) :: Fractional a => a -> a -> a
```

Haskell knows that we are using them as values of a type in typeclass **Fractional** here, because the / operator requires it.

We have talked about the numerical typeclasses and how they are subclasses of **Num**, but we have not talked about the actual types. We shall concentrate on three types, all instances of subclasses of **Num**. The first two are instances of **Integral**. These are **Integer** and **Int**. Numbers of type **Integer** represent any whole number, positive or negative or zero. Usually, these are the numbers we should like to use. However, for efficiency reasons, the type **Int** which uses numbers of limited size (at least -2^{29} to $2^{29} - 1$), also exists. We mention it only because it appears in the types of some simple built-in functions, like take, again for efficiency.

```
GHCi:
Prelude> :type take
take :: Int -> [a] -> [a]
```

Compare this with the type of our take' function, which is $(\textbf{Eq } a, \textbf{Num } a) \Rightarrow a \rightarrow [a] \rightarrow [a]$.

We have not seen **Int** or **Integer** before, because numerical functions in Haskell are often so general as to function with any instance of a typeclass such as **Num** or **Integral** or **Fractional**. And yet, if we are to make headway understanding Haskell's number system, we must address them in concrete terms. We can use the :: symbol to force Haskell to use a more specific type for a function. For example, we can define a function which adds any number, or just numbers which are of a type which is an instance of the **Integral** typeclass, or just things of type **Integer**:

```
GHCi:
Prelude> let f x y = x + y
Prelude> :type f
f :: Num a => a -> a -> a
Prelude> :{
Prelude| f :: Integral a => a -> a -> a
Prelude| f x y = x + y
Prelude| :}
Prelude> :{
Prelude| f :: Integer -> Integer -> Integer
Prelude| f x y = x + y
Prelude| :}
```

In this book we have not done this, and instead always allowed Haskell to infer the most general type possible. Here is another example: if we restrict a number to be of type **Integer**, we can no longer add it to a number with a decimal point in, because the two sides of the + sign must have the same type:

```
GHCi:
Prelude> x = 5 :: Integer
Prelude> :type x
x :: Integer
Prelude> x + 4.0

<interactive> error:
```

```
  • No instance for (Fractional Integer)
      arising from the literal '4.0'
  • In the second argument of '(+)', namely '4.0'
    In the expression: x + 4.0
    In an equation for 'it': it = x + 4.0
```

What is the type we have been using for real numbers? We have seen them with type **Num** a ⇒ a and type **Fractional** a ⇒ a, but we can give a more specific type, just as we did with **Int** and **Integer**:

```
GHCi:
Prelude> x = 5 :: Double
Prelude> x
5.0
```

A **Double** is a real number represented to relatively high-precision. The name is historical – its representation in the computer's memory takes twice as much space as a less precise representation of real numbers.

Sometimes it is necessary to convert between integers and real numbers, because we wish to use a function which applies only to integers or only to real numbers. The standard function fromInteger can convert an integer to a number of type **Num** a ⇒ a:

```
GHCi:
Prelude> x = 5 :: Integer
Prelude> y = fromInteger x
Prelude> :type fromInteger
fromInteger :: Num a => Integer -> a
```

Similarly, the function fromIntegral with type (**Integral** a, **Num** b) ⇒ a → b can convert any integral number to one of type **Num** a ⇒ a. How can we convert real numbers to integers? The function floor extracts the whole number part of a real number and returns it:

```
GHCi:
Prelude> floor 5.4
5
Prelude> :type floor
floor :: (Integral b, RealFrac a) => a -> b
```

Here we see one more typeclass, **RealFrac**, to complicate the story still further. The **RealFrac** typeclass is a subclass of **Fractional** which supplies rounding functions. Here is the new diagram:

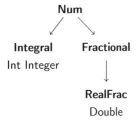

More on real numbers

It is clearly not possible to represent all numbers exactly – they might be irrational like π or e and have no finite representation. For most uses, a representation called *floating-point* is suitable, and this is how

Haskell's real numbers such as those of type **Double** are stored. Not all numbers can be represented exactly, but arithmetic operations are very quick.

```
GHCi:
Prelude> 1.5
1.5
Prelude> -2.3456
-2.3456
Prelude> 1 + 2.5 * 3.0
8.5
Prelude> 1 / 100000
1.0e-5
Prelude> 3000 ** 10
5.9049e34
Prelude> 3.123
3.123
Prelude> 3.123 - 3
0.12300000000000022
```

Exponentiation is written with the ∗∗ operator. Notice an example of the limits of precision in floating-point operations in the final lines. Note also that very small or very large numbers are written using scientific notation (such as 5.9049e+34 above).

Working with floating-point numbers requires care, and a comprehensive discussion is outside the scope of this book. These challenges exist in any programming language using the floating-point system. For example, evaluating 1. /. 0. gives the special value Infinity. There are other special values such as -Infinity and NaN ("not a number"). We will leave these complications for now – just be aware that they are lurking and must be confronted when writing robust numerical programs.

A number of standard functions are provided for operating on floating-point numbers, some of which are listed here:

Function	Type	Description
sqrt	**Floating** a ⇒ a → a	Square root of a number.
log	**Floating** a ⇒ a → a	Natural logarithm.
sin	**Floating** a ⇒ a → a	Sine of an angle, given in radians.
cos	**Floating** a ⇒ a → a	Cosine of an angle, given in radians.
tan	**Floating** a ⇒ a → a	Tangent of an angle, given in radians.
atan	**Floating** a ⇒ a → a	Arctangent of an angle, given in radians.

Another typeclass we have not seen before. It is for numbers for which trigonometric functions are defined. We can extend our diagram:

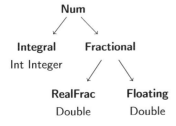

Let us write some functions with real numbers. We will write some simple operations on vectors in two dimensions. We will represent a point as a pair of numbers such as (2.5, 3). We will represent a vector as a pair of numbers too. Now we can write a function to build a vector from one point to another, one to find the length of a vector, one to offset a point by a vector, and one to scale a vector to a given length:

```
makeVector :: (Num a, Num b) ⇒ (a, b) → (a, b) → (a, b)
vectorLength :: Floating a ⇒ (a, a) → a
offsetPoint :: (Num a, Num b) ⇒ (a, b) → (a, b) → (a, b)
scaleToLength :: (Eq a, Floating a) ⇒ a → (a, a) → (a, a)

makeVector (x0, y0) (x1, y1) =
  (x1 - x0, y1 - y0)

vectorLength (x, y) =
  sqrt (x * x + y * y)

offsetPoint (x, y) (px, py) =
  (px + x, py + y)

scaleToLength l (a, b) =
  if currentLength == 0 then (a, b) else (a * factor, b * factor)
    where currentLength = vectorLength (a, b)
          factor = l / currentLength
```

Notice that some of our functions have fewer or different typeclass constraints than others.

Notice also that we have to be careful about division by zero. We have used tuples for the points because it is easier to read this way – we could have passed each number as a separate argument instead, of course.

Real numbers are often essential, but must be used with caution. You will discover this when answering the questions for this chapter. Some of these questions require using the built-in functions listed in the table above.

Adding more to the diagram

Some of the other typeclasses we have already seen, such as **Enum**, **Eq** and **Ord** can be placed in the diagram too:

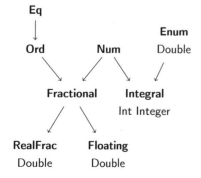

Note that **Num** is *not* a subclass of **Ord**, since not every number can be ordered along the number line – think, for example, of complex numbers.[1] Notice that we list in each part of the diagram only types which are direct instances of a typeclass. For example, **Int** is an instance of typeclass **Enum** by virtue of its being an instance of **Integral**, so it is not listed explicitly under **Enum**. In Question 6 you will be asked to add some of the other basic types we have seen to this diagram.

---

[1] Also, GHC differs from the Haskell 2010 standard: in standard Haskell, **Num** is a subclass of **Eq**. So you may see a slightly different diagram in other sources.

Questions

Hint: you may find yourself stuck trying to make types match with one another as you expect. Remembering the function `fromIntegral` will help with some of these questions.

1. Write a function to find the point midway between two given points in two dimensions.

2. Give a function `roundNum` which rounds a positive real number to the nearest whole number, returning is as another real number. You may use the built-in `ceiling` function, which is the opposite of the `floor` function.

3. Write a function to separate a real number into its whole and fractional parts. Return them as a tuple.

4. Write a function `star` of type which, given a number between zero and one, draws an asterisk to indicate the position. An argument of zero will result in an asterisk in column one, and an argument of one an asterisk in column fifty. Note that the special character `'\n'`, called a 'newline', moves onto the next line.

5. Now write a function `plot` which, given a function from numbers to numbers, a range, and a step size, uses `star` to draw a graph. For example, assuming the existence of the name pi for π, we might see:

```
GHCi:
Prelude> putStr (plot sin 0 pi (pi / 20))
*
         *
              *
                  *
                    *
                       *
                         *
                           *
                            *
                             *
                             *
                             *
                            *
                          *
                        *
                     *
                  *
               *
           *
        *
*
```

Here, we have plotted the sine function on the range $0 \ldots \pi$ in steps of size $\pi/20$. We shall discuss `putStr` in Chapter 14.

6. Add the **Bool** and **Char** types to our typeclass diagram.

So Far

1 Numbers ...-3 -2 -1 0 1 2 3...Booleans True and False. Characters like 'X' and '!'.

Mathematical operators + - * which take two numbers and give another.

Operators == < <= > >= /= which compare two values and evaluate to either True or False.

The "conditional" construct **if** *expression1* **then** *expression2* **else** *expression3*, where *expression1* evaluates to something boolean and *expression2* and *expression3* evaluate to the same sort of thing as one another.

The boolean operators && and || which allow us to build compound boolean expressions. The remainder operator `rem`.

2 Assigning a name to an expression using the *name = expression* construct. Building compound expressions using **let** *name1 = expression1* **in let** *name2 = expression2* **in** ...

Functions, introduced by *name argument1 argument2* ... = *expression*. These have type $a \rightarrow b$, $a \rightarrow b \rightarrow c$ etc. for some types a, b, c etc. Recursive functions. Turning a two-argument function into an operator with backticks like `rem`.

The types **Bool** and **Char**. The typeclasses **Num**, **Ord**, and **Eq**. A function from values of type a to type b with a in typeclass **Eq** and b in typeclass **Ord** would have type (**Eq** a, **Ord** b) $\Rightarrow$ a $\rightarrow$ b.

The special value it. The command :type and the use of Ctrl-C to interrupt a computation.

3 Matching patterns using f *pattern1* = *expression1* ↩ f *pattern2* = *expression2* etc... The expressions *expression1*, *expression2* etc. must have the same type as one another. Writing functions using guarded equations like f x | *guard* = *expression* ↩ | *guard2* = *expression2* | **otherwise** ... The typeclass **Integral**.

4 Lists, which are ordered collections of zero or more elements of like type. They are written between square brackets, with elements separated by commas e.g. [1, 2, 3, 4, 5]. If a list is non-empty, it has a head, which is its first element, and a tail, which is the list composed of the rest of the elements.

The : "cons" operator, which adds an element to the front of a list. The ++ "append" operator, which concatenates two lists together.

Using the : "cons" symbol for pattern matching to distinguish lists of length zero, one, etc. and their contents.

The shorthand list syntax [1 .. 10] and [1, 3 .. 10]. The typeclass **Enum**. List comprehensions [*expression* | *name* ← *list*, name2 ← *list2*, *guard*, *guard2*].

Strings, which are sequences of characters written between double quotes and are of type [**Char**] or **String**.

5 The `div` operator. The use of **where** as an alternative to **let**.

6 Anonymous functions *name* -> *expression*. Making operators into functions as in (<) and (+). The . function composition operator. Defining new operators.

7 The **Maybe** type with its constructors Nothing and Just. The **Either** type with its constructors Left and Right. The **case** ... **of** ... construct.

8 Tuples to combine a fixed number of elements (x, y), (x, y, z) etc. with types (a, b), (a, b, c) etc.

9 Partial application of functions by giving fewer than the full number of arguments. Operator sections like (10 /).

10 New types with **data**. The **Show** typeclass. Implementing **Show** automatically with **deriving**. The show function to create strings from things of other types.

12 Typeclasses **Fractional**, **Floating** and **RealFrac**. The types **Integer**, **Int**, and **Double**. Built-in functions on values of these types such as sin, sqrt, and log. Conversion functions like fromIntegral and floor.

Chapter 13

Being Lazy

Lists in Haskell can be infinitely long. For example, we can define a list recursively to consist of a head, followed by a tail equal to the list we are defining:

```
GHCi:
Prelude> ones = 1 : ones
```

This works, which perhaps we might not expect – if we are creating an infinitely-long list, why does the computer not just stall for ever? It is because Haskell is a *lazy* programming language, which means the elements of the list will only be calculated by ones when they are needed for the evaluation of another expression. Of course, if we try asking Haskell to print the list out, it does indeed go on forever, unless we interrupt it:

```
GHCi:
Prelude> ones = 1 : ones
Prelude> ones
[1,1,1,1,1,1,1,1,1,1,1,1,1,1,1,1,1^C1,1,1,Interrupted.
```

Remember we can interrupt a calculation with Ctrl-C . Here is a function to make any infinitely-long list with all elements the same:

```
repeat' :: a → [a]

repeat' x = x : repeat' x
```

Here is a function which can produce the infinitely-long list of numbers $n, n + 1, n + 2 \ldots$ for any given n:

```
from :: Num a ⇒ a → [a]

from x = x : from (x + 1)
```

Our usual `take'` function can be used to inspect the first part of the list:

```
GHCi:
Prelude> from x = x : from (x + 1)
Prelude> take' 20 (from 5)
[5,6,7,8,9,10,11,12,13,14,15,16,17,18,19,20,21,22,23,24]
```

Let us use `filter'` and `map'` to find the cubes divisible by five:

```
cubes :: Integral a ⇒ [a]

cubes =
    filter' (\x -> x `rem` 5 == 0) (map' (\x -> x * x * x) [1 ..])
```

Notice that the infinitely-long list can be made with `[1 ..]` rather than our `from` function. The type constraint is **Integral** (even though we use the `[ .. ]` construct) because **Integral** is a subclass of **Enum** so both need not be listed. Now, using `take'`:

```
GHCi:
Prelude> cubes = filter' (\x -> x `rem` 5 == 0) (map' (\x -> x * x * x) [1 ..])
Prelude> take' 20 cubes
[125,1000,3375,8000,15625,27000,42875,64000,91125,125000,166375,216000,
274625,343000,421875,512000,614125,729000,857375,1000000]
```

Of course, if no element is ever produced, `take'` can never return:

```
GHCi:
Prelude> take' 10 (filter' (\x -> x == 0) [1 ..])
^CInterrupted.
```

Here is another example of a simple lazy list, this time the list of all primes, created by use of `filter'` and recursion, beginning with the list of all numbers from 2:

```
makePrimes :: Integral a ⇒ [a] → [a]
primes :: Integral a ⇒ [a]

makePrimes (x:xs) =
    x : makePrimes (filter' (\n -> n `rem` x /= 0) xs)

primes = makePrimes [2 ..]
```

There are plenty of list functions which cannot be adapted to infinitely-long lists. We cannot, for example, reverse such a list, and appending two such lists does not make much sense. But there is an analogue to appending. We can combine two lists fairly, taking elements in turn from each:

```
interleave :: [a] → [a] → [a]

interleave (x:xs) ys = x : interleave ys xs
```

For example, using our `repeat'` function:

```
GHCi:
Prelude> take' 20 (interleave (repeat' 0) (repeat' 1))
[0,1,0,1,0,1,0,1,0,1,0,1,0,1,0,1,0,1,0,1]
```

We can use `interleave` to calculate the list of all lists of zeros and ones. We can do this by prepending a zero and a one to the list, and interleaving the resulting lists:

```
allFrom :: Num a ⇒ [a] → [[a]]
allLists :: Num a ⇒ [[a]]

allFrom l =
  l : interleave (allFrom (0 : l)) (allFrom (1 : l))

allLists = allFrom []
```

This yields:

```
GHCi:
Prelude> take' 20 allLists
[[],[0],[1],[0,0],[0,1],[1,0],[1,1],[0,0,0],[0,0,1],[0,1,0],[0,1,1],[1,0,0],
[1,0,1],[1,1,0],[1,1,1],[0,0,0,0],[0,0,0,1],[0,0,1,0],[0,0,1,1],[0,1,0,0]]
```

To see why, we can visualise the evaluation as a tree where each left branch prepends a zero and each right branch a one:

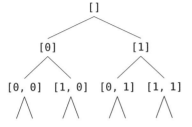

The interleavings are fair, and the interleavings of interleavings equally so, thus we see the results of length two in this order: [0, 0] [0, 1] [1, 0] [1, 1].

Questions

1. Write the list whose elements are the numbers $1, 2, 4, 8, 16 \ldots$

2. Write a function which, given a list, returns the list which consists of infinitely many copies of that list. For example, given the list [1, 2, 3] it should return a list with elements $1, 2, 3, 1, 2, 3, 1, 2 \ldots$

3. Write a list whose elements are the Fibonacci numbers $0, 1, 1, 2, 3, 5, 8 \ldots$ whose first two elements are zero and one by definition, and each ensuing element is the sum of the previous two.

4. Define an infinitely-branching tree containing the same data as allLists, but in the form of our tree diagram. Use a tree data type similar to that in Chapter 11. Write a function to make a list of the elements of such a tree.

5. Write the function unleave which, given a list, returns two lists, one containing elements at positions $0, 2, 4, 6 \ldots$ of the original list, and the other containing elements at positions $1, 3, 5, 7 \ldots$

So Far

1 Numbers ... -3 -2 -1 0 1 2 3... Booleans True and False. Characters like 'X' and '!'.

Mathematical operators + - * which take two numbers and give another.

Operators == < <= > >= /= which compare two values and evaluate to either True or False.

The "conditional" construct **if** *expression1* **then** *expression2* **else** *expression3*, where *expression1* evaluates to something boolean and *expression2* and *expression3* evaluate to the same sort of thing as one another.

The boolean operators && and || which allow us to build compound boolean expressions. The remainder operator `rem`.

2 Assigning a name to an expression using the *name = expression* construct. Building compound expressions using **let** *name1 = expression1* **in let** *name2 = expression2* **in** ...

Functions, introduced by *name argument1 argument2 ... = expression*. These have type $a \to b$, $a \to b \to c$ etc. for some types *a, b, c* etc. Recursive functions. Turning a two-argument function into an operator with backticks like `rem`.

The types **Bool** and **Char**. The typeclasses **Num, Ord,** and **Eq**. A function from values of type *a* to type *b* with *a* in typeclass **Eq** and *b* in typeclass **Ord** would have type (**Eq** a, **Ord** b) $\Rightarrow$ a $\to$ b.

The special value it. The command :type and the use of Ctrl-C to interrupt a computation.

3 Matching patterns using f *pattern1 = expression1* $\leftrightarrow$ f *pattern2 = expression2* etc... The expressions *expression1, expression2* etc. must have the same type as one another. Writing functions using guarded equations like f x | *guard = expression* $\leftrightarrow$ | *guard2 = expression2* | **otherwise** ... The typeclass **Integral**.

4 Lists, which are ordered collections of zero or more elements of like type. They are written between square brackets, with elements separated by commas e.g. [1, 2, 3, 4, 5]. If a list is non-empty, it has a head, which is its first element, and a tail, which is the list composed of the rest of the elements.

The : "cons" operator, which adds an element to the front of a list. The ++ "append" operator, which concatenates two lists together.

Using the : "cons" symbol for pattern matching to distinguish lists of length zero, one, etc. and their contents.

The shorthand list syntax [1 .. 10] and [1, 3 .. 10]. The typeclass **Enum**. List comprehensions [*expression* | name $\leftarrow$ *list*, name2 $\leftarrow$ *list2, guard, guard2*].

Strings, which are sequences of characters written between double quotes and are of type [**Char**] or **String**.

5 The `div` operator. The use of **where** as an alternative to **let**.

6 Anonymous functions *name -> expression*. Making operators into functions as in (<) and (+). The . function composition operator. Defining new operators.

7 The **Maybe** type with its constructors Nothing and Just. The **Either** type with its constructors Left and Right. The **case** ... **of** ... construct.

8 Tuples to combine a fixed number of elements (x, y), (x, y, z) etc. with types (a, b), (a, b, c) etc.

9 Partial application of functions by giving fewer than the full number of arguments. Operator sections like (10 /).

10 New types with **data**. The **Show** typeclass. Implementing **Show** automatically with **deriving**. The show function to create strings from things of other types.

12 Typeclasses **Fractional**, **Floating** and **RealFrac**. The types **Integer**, **Int**, and **Double**. Built-in functions on values of these types such as sin, sqrt, and log. Conversion functions like fromIntegral and floor.

13 The potentially infinitely-long list [*expression* ..].

Chapter 14

In and Out

We have considered a function (and indeed, a whole program composed of many functions) to take a piece of data, do some calculations, and then produce a result. This assumption has allowed us to write neat, easily understood programs.

However, some computer programs do not have all data available at the beginning of the program (or even the beginning of a given function). The user might provide new data interactively, or the program might fetch data from the internet, or two or more programs might communicate with one another in real time. Programs may wish to print to the screen, or read input from the user, halfway through their operation.

We must learn how to write such programs, whilst understanding the utility of restricting such complications to as small a part of the program as possible.

Writing to the screen

Haskell has a built-in function putStrLn which, if we use it within GHCi, results in the printing of a string to the screen:

```
GHCi:
Prelude> putStrLn "to the screen"
to the screen
Prelude>
```

The function putStr we used in Question 5 of Chapter 12 is similar but does not move to the next line. What is the type of putStrLn? Its argument is a **String**, but it is hard to see what it might return. Let us ask Haskell:

```
GHCi:
Prelude> :type putStrLn
putStrLn :: String -> IO ()
```

Well, the **String** part is as we expect. The right hand side, **IO** (), we have not seen before. The **IO** part tells us that this function returns an "IO action". The abbreviation **IO** is for Input/Output. The () part tells us that the **IO** action results in nothing (it just prints the string). Haskell has a special type to represent nothing, called (). So, the function putStrLn has type **String** → **IO** (). When we used the function, we gave it the string "to the screen", and it returned the **IO** action which, when run, prints that string to the screen but produces nothing.

It is GHCi running the **IO** action, not us calling the putStrLn function, which makes the words appear on the screen. This difference may not seem important, but we shall see later – particularly when we build self-contained programs rather than use GHCi – why it is.

How do we print something other than a string? As we have seen, Haskell has a function show which can convert other things into strings. For example:

```
GHCi:
Prelude> show 99
"99"
Prelude> show True
"True"
Prelude> show (1:2:[3])
"[1,2,3]"
```

Recall that the show function can turn anything into a **String** so long as its type is an instance of typeclass **Show**. We can build a compound **IO** action, to do one action after another, using the **do** construct. Here is a function which returns an **IO** action which, when run, prints out a single dictionary entry such as (**1**, "one") from our tree example, on two lines, using show:

```
printDictEntry :: Show a ⇒ (a, String) → IO ()

printDictEntry (k, v) =
  do putStrLn (show k)                          convert the key to a string
     putStrLn v
```

The **do** construct has allowed us to chain together a number of **IO** actions into one big one, so that their effects (such as printing to the screen) occur one after another in strict order when the **IO** action is run. Can you see why printDictEntry has the type it does? Let us see how printDictEntry is used in practice:

```
GHCi:
Prelude> printDictEntry (1, "one")
1
one
```

The distinction we drew between using a function which returns an **IO** action and having GHCi run the action for us, can be demonstrated by assigning a name to the result of the printDictEntry function:

```
GHCi:
Prelude> :type printDictEntry
printDictEntry :: Show a => (a, String) -> IO ()
Prelude> a = printDictEntry (1, "one")
Prelude> :type a
a :: IO ()
Prelude> a
1
one
```

How might we print a whole dictionary (represented as a list of entries) this way? Well, we can write a function to go over the entries one by one:

```
printDict :: Show a ⇒ [(a, String)] → IO ()

printDict [] = return ()                              nothing to do
printDict (x:xs) =
  do printDictEntry x                             print the first entry
     printDict xs                                      print the rest
```

The **return** construct is needed to make sure the right hand side of the first equation has type **IO** (), building an **IO** action which does nothing and results in ( ). Notice that the layout rule we introduced in Chapter 3 applies also to the **do** construct.

Reading from the keyboard

We can read a line from the keyboard using the `getLine` **IO** action. It returns the line as a string when we press the Enter key.

```
GHCi:
Prelude> getLine
What we've got here is a failure to communicate.
"What we've got here is a failure to communicate."
Prelude> :type getLine
getLine :: IO String
```

So `getLine` is not a function, but an **IO** action – it has no argument and no arrow in its type. When run, it will get its data from the keyboard not from our program. Since it is an **IO** action resulting in a string, its type is **IO String**. If we wish to keep the string, it is not sufficient to write, for example, x = `getLine`. This just makes x another name for `getLine`, rather than actually reading a line. We must use a different way – the <- construct. In this example the result of the `getLine` **IO** action is named `line`:

```
GHCi:
Prelude> line <- getLine
55
Prelude> line
"55"
Prelude> :type line
line :: String
```

The `getLine` **IO** action has been run for us by GHCi.

Now we should like to write an **IO** action `readDict` to read a dictionary typed in to the keyboard as a list of pairs of type [(**Integer**, **String**)]. To begin, we shall write an **IO** action which, when run, reads an integer from the keyboard. We shall need the built-in function `read` which can convert from a string to any type in typeclass **Read** that we give it (we shall choose the **Integer** type). Here is our `getInteger` **IO** action:

```
getInteger :: IO Integer

getInteger =
  do line <- getLine                           read the line and store it
     return (read line :: Integer)      convert to an integer and return
```

It has type **IO Integer** because it is an **IO** action which, when run, results in an integer. We want the user to enter a series of keys and values (integers and strings), one per line. They will enter zero for the integer to indicate no more input. Our **IO** action results in a dictionary of integers and strings, so its type will be **IO** [(**Integer**, **String**)]:

```
readDict :: IO [(Integer, String)]

readDict =
  do i <- getInteger                              read the integer
     if i == 0 then return [] else                no more entries
       do name <- getLine                         read the name
          dict <- readDict                read the rest of the dictionary
          return ((i, name) : dict)          return the whole dictionary
```

Notice that we must start a new **do** section inside the **else**. Notice also the use of **return** to build the **IO** action resulting in the empty list. We can ask GHCi to run this **IO** action and type in some suitable values:

```
GHCi:
Prelude> readDict
1
oak
2
ash
3
elm
0
[(1,"oak"),(2,"ash"),(3,"elm")]
```

But there is a problem. What happens if we type in something which is not an integer when an integer is expected?

```
GHCi:
Prelude> readDict
1
oak
ash
*** Exception: Prelude.read: no parse
```

The program cannot complete, because ash cannot be read as an integer by the read function. We need an alternative to the read function which does not fail in this manner.

Haskell provides the function readMaybe of type **Read** a ⇒ **String** → **Maybe** a (simple read has type **Read** a ⇒ **String** → a). So we can write the **IO** action getIntegerMaybe to read our integers, and extend readDict to use it, checking each result from getIntegerMaybe to see whether to ask the user to try again if a number cannot be read:

```
import Text.Read                         make the readMaybe function available

getIntegerMaybe :: IO (Maybe Integer)
readDictRobust :: IO [(Integer, String)]

getIntegerMaybe =
  do line <- getLine
      return (readMaybe line :: Maybe Integer)

readDictRobust =
  do i <- getIntegerMaybe
      case i of                          not case getIntegerMaybe of
        Just 0 -> return []                              finished
        Just x ->                           a valid number was entered
          do name <- getLine
              dict <- readDictRobust
              return ((x, name) : dict)
        Nothing ->                                   invalid number
          do putStrLn "Not a number. Try again."
              x <- readDictRobust
              return x
```

Functions such as `readMaybe` are not available by default, but must be *imported* using **import**. This is used to pick functions from those available, and make their named functions and types available. We do not want all the names available by default, because there are thousands of them, and many would clash will names we would like to use in our own programs. Let us import the Text.Read library which contains the readMaybe function:

```
GHCi:
Prelude> import Text.Read
Prelude Text.Read> :type readMaybe
readMaybe :: Read a => String -> Maybe a
```

Now let us try out our new program, seeing how typing mistakes can be fixed interactively:

```
Prelude Text.Read> readDictRobust
1
oak
ash
Not a number. Try again.
2
ash
3
elm
0
[(1,"oak"),(2,"ash"),(3,"elm")]
```

Using files

It is inconvenient to have to type new data sets in each time, so we will write functions to store a dictionary to a file, and then to read it back out again.

Haskell has some basic functions to help us read and write from places data can be stored, such as files. Let us import the System.IO library which contains the ones we will use. We are going to begin by writing a dictionary to a file, just like we wrote it to the screen. First, we shall need a function to open a file using the openFile function, and to close it using hClose:

GHCi:
```
Prelude> import System.IO                                    import functions from System.IO
Prelude System.IO> :type openFile
openFile :: FilePath -> IOMode -> IO Handle
Prelude System.IO> file <- openFile "dict.txt" WriteMode            open the file for writing
Prelude System.IO> :type file
file :: Handle
Prelude System.IO> :type hClose
hClose :: Handle -> IO ()
Prelude System.IO> hClose file                                              close the file
```

The type Handle is used to represent a file once it has been opened. The type FilePath is just another name for **String**, and the type IOMode consists of things like WriteMode and ReadMode to signify what kind of file action we will be doing. Now we can use hPutStrLn, which writes a line to the file represented by a given handle, to write our whole program:

```
import System.IO

entryToHandle :: Show a ⇒ Handle → (a, String) → IO ()
dictionaryToHandle :: Show a ⇒ Handle → [(a, String)] → IO ()
dictionaryToFile :: Show a ⇒ FilePath → [(a, String)] → IO ()

entryToHandle fh (k, v) =
  do hPutStrLn fh (show k)
     hPutStrLn fh v

dictionaryToHandle fh [] = return ()
dictionaryToHandle fh (x:xs) =
  do entryToHandle fh x
     dictionaryToHandle fh xs

dictionaryToFile filename dict =
  do fh <- openFile filename WriteMode
     dictionaryToHandle fh dict
     hClose fh
```

We have chosen the abbreviation fh instead of, for example, fileHandle for brevity. After using this function, and after GHCi runs the resultant **IO** action, you should find a file of the chosen name on your computer in the same folder from which you are running Haskell. In the following example, we are reading a dictionary from the user and writing it to file as file.txt:

GHCi:
```
Prelude System.IO Text.Read> dict <- readDictRobust
1
oak
```

```
2
ash
3
elm
0
Prelude System.IO Text.Read> dict
[(1,"oak"),(2,"ash"),(3,"elm")]
Prelude System.IO Text.Read> dictionaryToFile "file.txt" dict
```

Now we have written a file, we can read it back in using the functions hGetLine and the IOMode ReadMode:

```
import System.IO
import Text.Read

entryOfHandle :: Handle → IO (Maybe (Integer, String))
dictionaryOfHandle :: Handle → IO (Maybe [(Integer, String)])
dictionaryOfFile :: FilePath → IO (Maybe [(Integer, String)])

entryOfHandle fh =
  do k <- hGetLine fh
     v <- hGetLine fh
     case readMaybe k :: Maybe Integer of
       Nothing -> return Nothing
       Just k' -> return (Just (k', v))

dictionaryOfHandle fh =
  do ended <- hIsEOF fh
     if ended then return (Just []) else
     do x <- entryOfHandle fh
        case x of
          Nothing -> return Nothing
          Just x' ->
            do xs <- dictionaryOfHandle fh
               case xs of
                 Nothing -> return Nothing
                 Just xs' -> return (Just (x' : xs'))

dictionaryOfFile fileName =
  do fh <- openFile fileName ReadMode
     dict <- dictionaryOfHandle fh
     hClose fh
     return dict
```

Notice that the functions all return **IO** actions involving a **Maybe** type – the file may not contain a valid dictionary.

GHCi:
```
Prelude> import System.IO
Prelude System.IO> import Text.Read
Prelude System.IO Text.Read> dictionaryOfFile "file.txt"
Just [(1,"oak"),(2,"ash"),(3,"elm")]
```

We have introduced **IO**, (), Handle, and IOMode for file input/output. Here are the functions we have used:

Function	Type	Description
openFile	FilePath → IOMode → **IO** Handle	Open a file for reading or writing.
hClose	Handle → **IO** ()	Close a file.
hPutStrLn	Handle → **String** → **IO** ()	Write a line to a file which has been opened for writing.
hGetLine	Handle → **IO String**	Read a line from a file which has been opened for reading.
hIsEOF	Handle → **IO Bool**	Check if we have reached the end of a file opened for reading.

Example: text file statistics

We are going to write a program to count the number of words, sentences and lines in a text file. We shall consider the opening paragraph of Kafka's "Metamorphosis".

```
One morning, when Gregor Samsa woke from troubled dreams, he found
himself transformed in his bed into a horrible vermin.  He lay on
his armour-like back, and if he lifted his head a little he could
see his brown belly, slightly domed and divided by arches into stiff
sections.  The bedding was hardly able to cover it and seemed ready
to slide off any moment.  His many legs, pitifully thin compared
with the size of the rest of him, waved about helplessly as he
looked.
```

There are newline characters at the end of each line, save for the last. You can cut and paste or type this into a text file to try these examples out. Here, it is saved as gregor.txt.

We will just count lines first. To this, we will write a function handleStatistics to gather the statistics by reading from a file handle and then print them. Then we will have a function fileStatistics to open a named file, call our first function, and close it again. (Notice that we will now use the shorthand "a function to…" to mean "a function which returns an **IO** action which, when run, will…").

```
import System.IO

handleStatistics :: (Show a, Num a) ⇒ Handle → a → IO ()
fileStatistics :: FilePath → IO ()

handleStatistics fh lines =
  do ended <- hIsEOF fh
     if ended then
       do putStr "There were "
          putStr (show lines)
          putStrLn " lines."
     else
       do line <- hGetLine fh
          handleStatistics fh (lines + 1)

fileStatistics filename =
  do fh <- openFile filename ReadMode
     handleStatistics fh 0
     hClose fh
```

Using our function with our example file results in the following output:

```
GHCi:
Prelude System.IO> fileStatistics "gregor.txt"
There were 8 lines.
```

Let us update the program to count the number of words, characters, and sentences. We will do this simplistically, assuming that the number of words can be counted by counting the number of spaces, and that the sentences can be counted by noting instances of '.', '!', and '?'. We can extend the handleStatistics function appropriately – the fileStatistics function need not change:

```
import System.IO

handleStatistics ::
    (Show a, Show b, Show c, Show d, Num a, Num b, Num c, Num d) ⇒
    Handle → a → b → c → d → IO ()
fileStatistics :: FilePath → IO ()

handleStatistics fh lines characters words sentences =
  do ended <- hIsEOF fh
     if ended then
       do putStr "There were "
          putStr (show lines)
          putStr " lines, making up "
          putStr (show characters)
          putStr " characters with "
          putStr (show words)
          putStr " words in "
          putStr (show sentences)
          putStrLn " sentences."
     else
       do line <- hGetLine fh
          let charCount = length' line
              wordCount = length' (filter' (\x -> x == ' ') line)
              sentenceCount =
                length' (filter'
                             (\x -> x == '.' || x == '?' || x == '!')
                             line)
          handleStatistics
            fh (lines + 1) (characters + charCount)
            (words + wordCount) (sentences + sentenceCount)

fileStatistics fileName =
  do fh <- openFile fileName ReadMode
     handleStatistics fh 0 0 0 0
     hClose fh
```

Notice that we can use **let** without **in** to introduce new names in a **do** construct. Substituting this version of handleStatistics (if you are cutting and pasting into GHCi, be sure to also paste fileStatistics in again afterwards, so it uses the new handleStatistics), gives the following result on our example text:

```
GHCi:
Prelude System.IO> fileStatistics "gregor.txt"
There were 8 lines, making up 464 characters with 80 words in 4 sentences.
```

Adding character counts

We should like to build a histogram, counting the number of times each letter of the alphabet or other character occurs. We can use the binary search tree implementation of the dictionary data structure we introduced in Chapter 11 for this. The keys are the characters, and the values are the counts. Here is the function to add or update a histogram entry:

```
updateHistogram :: (Ord a, Num b) ⇒ Tree (a, b) → [a] → Tree (a, b)

updateHistogram tr [] = tr
updateHistogram tr (x:xs) =
  case lookup tr x of
    Nothing ->
      updateHistogram (treeInsert tr x 1) xs
    Just v ->
      updateHistogram (treeInsert tr x (v + 1)) xs
```

If there is not an entry in the dictionary, we initialise the counter at one, otherwise, we add one to the counter. Our main function is getting rather long, so we will write a separate one which, given the completed tree prints out the frequencies. We shall sort them alphabetically. We use the functions mergeSort and listOfTree from earlier in the book to help us here.

```
printHistogramList :: (Show a, Show b) ⇒ [(a, b)] → IO ()
printHistogram :: (Show a, Show b, Ord a, Ord b) ⇒ Tree (a, b) → IO ()

printHistogramList [] = return ()
printHistogramList ((k, v):xs) =
  do putStr "For character "
     putStr (show k)
     putStr " the count is "
     putStr (show v)
     putStrLn "."
     printHistogramList xs

printHistogram tree =
  printHistogramList (mergeSort (listOfTree tree))
```

For example, here is a line of output from printHistogram:

```
For character 'd' the count is 6.
```

We update handleStatistics to keep the histogram, and to print it with the other information when we are finished. The fileStatistics function must also be updated to create the empty histogram.

```
import System.IO

handleStatistics ::
    (Show a, Show b, Show c, Show d, Num a, Num b, Num c, Num d) ⇒
    Handle → a → b → c → d → Tree (Char, Integer) → IO ()
fileStatistics :: FilePath → IO ()

handleStatistics fh lines characters words sentences histogram =
  do ended <- hIsEOF fh
     if ended then
        do putStr "There were "
           putStr (show lines)
           putStr " lines, making up "
           putStr (show characters)
           putStr " characters with "
           putStr (show words)
           putStr " words in "
           putStr (show sentences)
           putStrLn " sentences."
           printHistogram histogram
     else
        do line <- hGetLine fh
           let charCount = length' line
               wordCount = length' (filter' (\x -> x == ' ') line)
               sentenceCount =
                 length'
                   (filter' (\x -> x == '.' || x == '?' || x == '!')
                   line)
               histogram' = updateHistogram histogram line
           handleStatistics
             fh (lines + 1) (characters + charCount)
             (words + wordCount) (sentences + sentenceCount)
             histogram'

fileStatistics fileName =
  do fh <- openFile fileName ReadMode
     handleStatistics fh 0 0 0 0 Lf
     hClose fh
```

Here is the output on our text:

```
GHCi:
Prelude> fileStatistics "gregor.txt"
There were 8 lines, making up 464 characters with 80 words in 4 sentences.
Character frequencies:
For character ' ' the count is 80.
For character ',' the count is 6.
For character '-' the count is 1.
For character '.' the count is 4.
For character 'G' the count is 1.
```

```
For character 'H' the count is 2.
For character 'O' the count is 1.
For character 'S' the count is 1.
For character 'T' the count is 1.
For character 'a' the count is 24.
For character 'b' the count is 10.
For character 'c' the count is 6.
For character 'd' the count is 25.
For character 'e' the count is 47.
For character 'f' the count is 13.
For character 'g' the count is 5.
For character 'h' the count is 22.
For character 'i' the count is 30.
For character 'k' the count is 4.
For character 'l' the count is 23.
For character 'm' the count is 15.
For character 'n' the count is 21.
For character 'o' the count is 27.
For character 'p' the count is 3.
For character 'r' the count is 20.
For character 's' the count is 24.
For character 't' the count is 21.
For character 'u' the count is 6.
For character 'v' the count is 4.
For character 'w' the count is 6.
For character 'y' the count is 10.
For character 'z' the count is 1.
```

The most common character is the space. The most common alphabetic character is `'e'`.

Questions

1. Write a function to build an **IO** action which, when run, prints a list of numbers to the screen in the same format Haskell uses – i.e. with square brackets and commas, using the show function only on individual elements (not on the whole list).

2. Write an **IO** action to read three integers from the user, and return them as a tuple. What problems could occur in the process? Handle them appropriately.

3. In our readDict **IO** action, we waited for the user to type 0 to indicate no more data. This is clumsy. Implement a new readDict function with a nicer system.

4. Write a function which, given a number x, returns an **IO** action which, when run, prints the x-times table to a given file name. For example, table "table.txt" 5 should result in a file table.txt containing the following:

1	2	3	4	5
2	4	6	8	10
3	6	9	12	15
4	8	12	16	20
5	10	15	20	25

   Adding the special tabulation character '\t' after each number will line up the columns.

5. Write a function to count the number of lines in a given file.

6. Write a function copyFile of type FilePath → FilePath → **IO** () which returns an **IO** action which copies a file line by line. Remember that a FilePath is just another name for **String**. For example, copyFile "a.txt" "b.txt" should produce a file b.txt identical to a.txt. Make sure you deal with the case where the file a.txt cannot be found, or where b.txt cannot be created or filled.

7. Comment on the accuracy of our character, word, line, and sentence statistics in the case of our example paragraph. What about in general?

8. Choose one of the problems you have identified, and modify our program to fix it.

So Far

1 Numbers ...-3 -2 -1 0 1 2 3...Booleans True and False. Characters like 'X' and '!'.

Mathematical operators + - * which take two numbers and give another.

Operators == < <= > >= /= which compare two values and evaluate to either True or False.

The "conditional" construct **if** *expression1* **then** *expression2* **else** *expression3*, where *expression1* evaluates to something boolean and *expression2* and *expression3* evaluate to the same sort of thing as one another.

The boolean operators && and || which allow us to build compound boolean expressions. The remainder operator `rem`.

2 Assigning a name to an expression using the *name = expression* construct. Building compound expressions using **let** *name1 = expression1* **in let** *name2 = expression2* **in** ...

Functions, introduced by *name argument1 argument2 ... = expression*. These have type $a \rightarrow b$, $a \rightarrow b \rightarrow c$ etc. for some types a, b, c etc. Recursive functions. Turning a two-argument function into an operator with backticks like `rem`.

The types **Bool** and **Char**. The typeclasses **Num**, **Ord**, and **Eq**. A function from values of type a to type b with a in typeclass **Eq** and b in typeclass **Ord** would have type (**Eq** a, **Ord** b) $\Rightarrow$ a $\rightarrow$ b.

The special value it. The command :type and the use of Ctrl-C to interrupt a computation.

3 Matching patterns using f *pattern1 = expression1* $\longleftrightarrow$ f *pattern2 = expression2* etc... The expressions *expression1, expression2* etc. must have the same type as one another. Writing functions using guarded equations like f x | *guard = expression* $\longleftrightarrow$ | *guard2 = expression2* | **otherwise** ... The typeclass **Integral**.

4 Lists, which are ordered collections of zero or more elements of like type. They are written between square brackets, with elements separated by commas e.g. [1, 2, 3, 4, 5]. If a list is non-empty, it has a head, which is its first element, and a tail, which is the list composed of the rest of the elements.

The : "cons" operator, which adds an element to the front of a list. The ++ "append" operator, which concatenates two lists together.

Using the : "cons" symbol for pattern matching to distinguish lists of length zero, one, etc. and their contents.

The shorthand list syntax [1 .. 10] and [1, 3 .. 10]. The typeclass **Enum**. List comprehensions [*expression* | *name* $\leftarrow$ *list*, *name2* $\leftarrow$ *list2, guard, guard2*].

Strings, which are sequences of characters written between double quotes and are of type [**Char**] or **String**.

5 The `div` operator. The use of **where** as an alternative to **let**.

6 Anonymous functions *name -> expression*. Making operators into functions as in (<) and (+). The . function composition operator. Defining new operators.

7 The **Maybe** type with its constructors Nothing and Just. The **Either** type with its constructors Left and Right. The **case** ... **of** ... construct.

8 Tuples to combine a fixed number of elements (x, y), (x, y, z) etc. with types (a, b), (a, b, c) etc.

9 Partial application of functions by giving fewer than the full number of arguments. Operator sections like (10 /).

10 New types with **data**. The **Show** typeclass. Implementing **Show** automatically with **deriving**. The show function to create strings from things of other types.

12 Typeclasses **Fractional**, **Floating** and **RealFrac**. The types **Integer**, **Int**, and **Double**. Built-in functions on values of these types such as sin, sqrt, and log. Conversion functions like fromIntegral and floor.

13 The potentially infinitely-long list [*expression* ..].

14 Input/output actions **IO**. The value () of type (). Performing input/output actions with **do** and <- and **return**. Using **let** without in to introduce new names. The **Read** typeclass. FilePath, Handle and two sorts of IOMode: ReadMode and WriteMode. Importing a module with **import**.

Chapter 15

Building Bigger Programs

So far we have been writing little programs and testing them interactively in GHCi. However, to conquer the complexity of the task of writing larger programs, tools are needed to split them into well-defined *modules*, each with a given set of types and functions. We can then build big systems without worrying that some internal change to a single module will affect the whole program. This process of modularization is known as *abstraction*, and is fundamental to writing large programs, a discipline sometimes called software engineering.

In this chapter, you will have to create text files and type commands into the command prompt of your computer. If you are not sure how to do this, or the examples in this chapter do not work for you, ask a friend or teacher. In particular, if using Microsoft Windows, some of the commands may have different names.

Making a module

We will be building a modular version of our text statistics program from Chapter 14. First, write the text file shown in Figure 15.1 (but not the italic annotations) and save it as TextStat.hs (Haskell modules live in files ending in .hs and have an initial capital letter).

The first line is a comment. Comments in Haskell are written after two - - hyphens. We use comments in large programs to help the reader (who might be someone else, or ourselves some time later) to understand the program. The second line, **module** Textstat **where**, introduces a name for the module we are defining. It is the same as the first part of the file name, but with an initial capital letter.

We have then introduced a type for our statistics using the **type** construct. This is a *type abbreviation*, rather than a new type like we might introduce with **data**. It means we can use the name Stats instead of writing (Integer, Integer, Integer, Integer). This will hold the number of words, characters, and sentences. We have then written a function statsFromChannel which produces the statistics. A final function statsFromFile can open a file and use statsFromChannel on it.

We can load and use this module in GHCi using the :load command:

```
GHCi:
Prelude> :load TextStat.hs
[1 of 1] Compiling TextStat        ( TextStat.hs, interpreted )
Ok, one module loaded.
*TextStat> statsFromFile "gregor.txt"
(8,464,80,4)
```

```
-- Text statistics                                              comment

module Textstat where                                  define a new module

import System.IO                          for access to file reading functions

type Stats = (Integer, Integer, Integer, Integer)       the type abbreviation

length' :: Num b => [a] -> b

length' [] = 0
length' (_:xs) = 1 + length' xs

statsFromChannel :: Handle -> Stats -> IO Stats

statsFromChannel fh (lines, characters, words, sentences) =
  do ended <- hIsEOF fh
     if ended then
       return (lines, characters, words, sentences)
     else
       do line <- hGetLine fh
          let charCount = length' line
              wordCount = length' (filter' (\x -> x == ' ') line)
              sentenceCount =
                length'
                  (filter'
                    (\x -> x == '.' || x == '?'|| x == '!')
                    line)
          statsFromChannel
            fh
            ((lines + 1),
            (characters + charCount),
            (words + wordCount),
            (sentences + sentenceCount))

statsFromFile :: FilePath -> IO Stats

statsFromFile filename =
  do fh <- openFile filename ReadMode
     result <- statsFromChannel fh (0, 0, 0, 0)
     hClose fh
     return result
```

Figure 15.1: TextStat.hs

Building standalone programs

We can issue a command to turn this program into a pre-processed Haskell module. This *compiles* the program. Execute the following command:

```
ghc TextStat.hs
```

You can see that the name of the Haskell compiler we are using is ghc. If there are errors in TextStat.hs they will be printed out, including the line and character number of the problem. You must fix these, and try the command again. If compilation succeeds, you will see the files TextStat.hi and TextStat.o in the current folder.

We cannot use these new files directly. Let us add another file Stats.hs which will use functions from the TextStat module to create a program which, when given a file name, prints some statistics about it. This is illustrated in Figure 15.2. There are two new things here:

1. The place where the program is to start must be called main, and it is an IO action of type IO (). When we use our program from the command line, this IO action will be run.

2. We use the getArgs IO action from System.Environment to get a list of strings representing the "arguments" to our program, that is the things we type on the command line after the name of the program.

Let us compile this standalone program using ghc:

```
ghc TextStat.hs Stats.hs
```

Now, we can run the program:

```
$ ./Stats gregor.txt
Words: 80
Characters: 464
Sentences: 4
Lines: 8

$ ./Stats not_there.txt
Stats: not_there.txt: openFile: does not exist (No such file or directory)

$ ./Stats
Usage: Stats <filename>
```

This output might look slightly different on your computer.

```
-- Text Statistics main program

import System.Environment
import Textstat

main :: IO ()                                          the main program is an IO action

main =
  do args <- getArgs                                       fetch the arguments
     case args of
       [infile] ->                                      just one, the file name
         do (l, c, w, s) <- Textstat.statsFromFile infile
            putStr "Lines: "
            putStrLn (show l)
            putStr "Characters: "
            putStrLn (show c)
            putStr "Words: "
            putStrLn (show w)
            putStr "Sentences: "
            putStrLn (show s)
       _ -> putStrLn "Usage: Stats <filename>"
```

Figure 15.2: Stats.hs

Questions

1. Extend our example to print the character histogram data as we did in Chapter 14.

2. Write a standalone program to reverse the lines in a text file, writing to another file.

3. Write a program to print out the size of a given file. That is to say, the number of characters in the file.

4. Write and compile a standalone program to sort a list of numbers given in a file. The file will have one number per line. The sorted list should be written to a second file.

5. Write a standalone program using your `copyFile` function from the question to Chapter 14. We can then execute the command `CopyFile a.txt b.txt` on the command line to copy the file `a.txt` to `b.txt`.

6. Write a standalone program to search for a given string in a file. Lines where the string is found should be printed to the screen.

So Far

1 Numbers ... -3 -2 -1 0 1 2 3...Booleans True and False. Characters like 'X' and '!'.

Mathematical operators + - * which take two numbers and give another.

Operators == < <= > >= /= which compare two values and evaluate to either True or False.

The "conditional" construct **if** *expression1* **then** *expression2* **else** *expression3*, where *expression1* evaluates to something boolean and *expression2* and *expression3* evaluate to the same sort of thing as one another.

The boolean operators && and || which allow us to build compound boolean expressions. The remainder operator `rem`.

2 Assigning a name to an expression using the *name = expression* construct. Building compound expressions using **let** *name1 = expression1* **in let** *name2 = expression2* **in** ...

Functions, introduced by *name argument1 argument2 ... = expression*. These have type $a \rightarrow b$, $a \rightarrow b \rightarrow c$ etc. for some types a, b, c etc. Recursive functions. Turning a two-argument function into an operator with backticks like `rem`.

The types **Bool** and **Char**. The typeclasses **Num**, **Ord**, and **Eq**. A function from values of type a to type b with a in typeclass **Eq** and b in typeclass **Ord** would have type (**Eq** a, **Ord** b) $\Rightarrow$ a $\rightarrow$ b.

The special value it. The command :type and the use of Ctrl-C to interrupt a computation.

3 Matching patterns using f *pattern1 = expression1* ↩ f *pattern2 = expression2* etc... The expressions *expression1*, *expression2* etc. must have the same type as one another. Writing functions using guarded equations like f x | *guard = expression* ↩ | *guard2 = expression2* | **otherwise** ... The typeclass **Integral**.

4 Lists, which are ordered collections of zero or more elements of like type. They are written between square brackets, with elements separated by commas e.g. [1, 2, 3, 4, 5]. If a list is non-empty, it has a head, which is its first element, and a tail, which is the list composed of the rest of the elements.

The : "cons" operator, which adds an element to the front of a list. The ++ "append" operator, which concatenates two lists together.

Using the : "cons" symbol for pattern matching to distinguish lists of length zero, one, etc. and their contents.

The shorthand list syntax [1 .. 10] and [1, 3 .. 10]. The typeclass **Enum**. List comprehensions [*expression* | *name ← list*, *name2 ← list2*, *guard*, *guard2*].

Strings, which are sequences of characters written between double quotes and are of type [**Char**] or **String**.

5 The `div` operator. The use of **where** as an alternative to **let**.

6 Anonymous functions *name -> expression*. Making operators into functions as in (<) and (+). The . function composition operator. Defining new operators.

7 The **Maybe** type with its constructors Nothing and Just. The **Either** type with its constructors Left and Right. The **case** ... **of** ... construct.

8 Tuples to combine a fixed number of elements (x, y), (x, y, z) etc. with types (a, b), (a, b, c) etc.

9 Partial application of functions by giving fewer than the full number of arguments. Operator sections like (10 /).

10 New types with **data**. The **Show** typeclass. Implementing **Show** automatically with **deriving**. The show function to create strings from things of other types.

12 Typeclasses **Fractional**, **Floating** and **RealFrac**. The types **Integer**, **Int**, and **Double**. Built-in functions on values of these types such as sin, sqrt, and log. Conversion functions like fromIntegral and floor.

13 The potentially infinitely-long list [*expression* ..].

14 Input/output actions **IO**. The value () of type (). Performing input/output actions with **do** and <- and **return**. Using **let** without **in** to introduce new names. The **Read** typeclass. FilePath, Handle and two sorts of IOMode: ReadMode and WriteMode. Importing a module with **import**.

15 The ghc command for compiling programs. Writing comments with --. Defining a module with **module** *name* **where**. Type abbreviations with **type**. Defining the main **IO** action with main. Getting command line arguments with getArgs.

Chapter 16

The Standard Prelude and Base

We can divide the words and symbols we have been using to build Haskell programs into four kinds:

1. The language itself. For example, words like **let** and **where**.

2. Things which are not part of the language, but which are always available, such as show and getLine. These also include operators like &&. These things form what is called the *Standard Prelude*, because they are automatically loaded (hence standard) before (hence prelude) our program.

3. Things we had to ask for specifically by using **import**. These are extra modules supplied with Haskell, called the *Base*. The Base includes the Standard Prelude, which is imported by default.

4. Definitions from modules we have built ourselves, such as Textstat in the preceding chapter.

This chapter is about the second and third categories. Many of the functions we have learned how to write in this book are, in fact, supplied in the Standard Prelude. Here they are, together with their equivalents:

Chapter	Our function	In the Standard Prelude	Description
2	gcd'	gcd	greatest common divisor
2	not'	not	logical negation
2	sum'	sum	sum of a list
4	length'	length	length of a list
4	take'	take	take elements from the front of a list
4	drop'	drop	drop elements from the front of a list
4	elem'	elem	membership test on a list
4	reverse'	reverse	reverse a list
6	map'	map	process a list
6	all'	all	all element satisfy a predicate
8	fst'	fst	first element of a pair
8	snd'	snd	second element of a pair
8	lookup'	lookup	look up an item in a dictionary
11	max'	max	larger of two numbers
12	replicate'	replicate	multiple copies in a list
13	repeat'	repeat	build infinitely-long list from single item

Why did we give them different names? Haskell will not let us redefine a name which has been used before in a .hs script. For example, if we define the lookup function for looking up an item in a dictionary and try to compile it, we see an error:

```
$ ghc Program.hs
[1 of 1] Compiling Main              ( Program.hs, Program.o )

program.hs:3:7: error:
    Ambiguous occurrence 'lookup'
    It could refer to either 'Prelude.lookup',
                    imported from 'Prelude' at Program.hs:1:1
                    (and originally defined in 'GHC.List')
        or 'Main.lookup', defined at Program.hs:1:1
```

This policy is rather strict, but it helps to rule out bugs caused by inadvertently using the wrong function. The message also tells us where in the .hs file the error is located – here at line 3, column 7. Note also that some of the types for the Standard Prelude versions of the functions are different, and may contain words we have not seen yet. But they may be used in much the same way. Here are the functions with differing types:

Function	Our type	Standard Prelude type
take	$(\textbf{Eq } a, \textbf{Num } a) \Rightarrow a \rightarrow [b] \rightarrow [b]$	$\textbf{Int} \rightarrow [a] \rightarrow [a]$
drop	$(\textbf{Eq } a, \textbf{Num } a) \Rightarrow a \rightarrow [b] \rightarrow [b]$	$\textbf{Int} \rightarrow [a] \rightarrow [a]$
replicate	$(\textbf{Eq } a, \textbf{Num } a) \Rightarrow a \rightarrow b \rightarrow [b]$	$\textbf{Int} \rightarrow a \rightarrow [a]$
sum	$\textbf{Num } a \Rightarrow [a] \rightarrow a$	$(\textbf{Num } a, \textbf{Foldable } b) \Rightarrow b\ a \rightarrow a$
length	$\textbf{Num } a \Rightarrow [b] \rightarrow a$	$\textbf{Foldable } b \Rightarrow b\ a \Rightarrow \textbf{Int}$
elem	$\textbf{Eq } a \Rightarrow a \rightarrow [a] \rightarrow \textbf{Bool}$	$(\textbf{Eq } a, \textbf{Foldable } b) \Rightarrow a \rightarrow b\ a \rightarrow \textbf{Bool}$
all	$(a \rightarrow \textbf{Bool}) \rightarrow [a] \rightarrow \textbf{Bool}$	$\textbf{Foldable } b \Rightarrow (a \rightarrow \textbf{Bool}) \rightarrow b\ a \rightarrow \textbf{Bool}$

There are two differences here. First, the functions take, drop, replicate, and length use the type **Int** for the argument which is always a number. This is for reasons of efficiency. The second difference is the use of the typeclass **Foldable**. This is a way to write functions which operate not only over lists, but other kinds of data structures as well, in a consistent way. You may use, for example, length just as you use the length' function we wrote. Some functions may differ slightly. For example, take' 3 [1] returns [1] rather than failing to complete.

Outside of the Standard Prelude, we have used things from the following modules from the Base:

Module	Description	Functions and names we used
System.IO	Input/Output	openFile, ReadMode, WriteMode, hIsEOF, hClose
System.Environment	Program's environment	getArgs
Text.Read	Reading text	readMaybe

The Base documentation is supplied with Haskell, or may be consulted online. Here, for example, is the documentation for the Standard Prelude map function:

```
map :: (a -> b) -> [a] -> [b]

    map f xs is the list obtained by applying f to each element of xs, i.e.,

    map f [x1, x2, ..., xn] == [f x1, f x2, ..., f xn]
    map f [x1, x2, ...]  == [f x1, f x2, ...]
```

In order to answer the questions for this chapter, please have on hand a copy of the Haskell documentation.

Some sins of omission

Haskell as practised can be a language of some complexity, and we have had to tread carefully in this introductory text. Time to repent. The word **return**, though we wrote it in bold type, is not really a special word, but simply a function in the Standard Prelude:

```
GHCi:
Prelude> :type return
return :: Monad m => a -> m a
```

We did not mention this because of the unfamiliar type. For a similar reason, when we wrote functions to do input/output, we often wrote a function which repeatedly used another:

```
printDictEntry :: Show a ⇒ (a, String) → IO ()
printDict :: Show a ⇒ [(a, String)] → IO ()

printDictEntry (k, v) =
   do putStrLn (show k)
      putStrLn v

printDict [] = return ()
printDict (x:xs) =
   do printDictEntry x
      printDict xs
```

A nicer solution is to write a generic function doList:

```
doList :: Monad m ⇒ (t → m a) → [t] → m ()
printDict :: Show a ⇒ [(a, String)] → IO ()

doList _ [] = return ()
doList f (x:xs) =
   do f x
      doList f xs

printDict = doList printDictEntry
```

This can then be reused at will. In fact, the Standard Prelude has a similar function, again with part of its type we do not yet understand:

```
GHCi:
Prelude> :type mapM_
mapM_ :: (Foldable t, Monad m) => (a -> m b) -> t a -> m ()
```

You may use this function for now without understanding its type. But these are matters for quite another book.

Questions

1. Use a function from the Data.Char module to write a function which replaces all upper case characters in a given string with lower case ones.

2. Use the functions dropWhile and takeWhile to isolate the first section of a list which contains positive numbers. For example, isolate [-6, -4, -1, 0, 1, 2, 4, 5, 3, 2, -1, -9] should yield the list [1, 2, 4, 5, 3, 2].

3. The word **otherwise** for guarded equations is not really part of the Haskell language, but is defined in the Standard Prelude. Find or deduce its definition.

4. Use functions from Data.String to write a program which reverses the order of the words in its input string.

5. The functions ord (short for ordinal) and chr (short for character) from the Data.Char module convert between numbers and characters (each character has an associated number). Use these functions to write a function toLower which converts an upper case letter to lower case, leaving any other character alone. This is a home-made version of the function you used to solve Question 1 above.

So Far

1 Numbers ...-3 -2 -1 0 1 2 3...Booleans True and False. Characters like 'X' and '!'.

Mathematical operators + - * which take two numbers and give another.

Operators == < <= > >= /= which compare two values and evaluate to either True or False.

The "conditional" construct **if** *expression1* **then** *expression2* **else** *expression3*, where *expression1* evaluates to something boolean and *expression2* and *expression3* evaluate to the same sort of thing as one another.

The boolean operators && and || which allow us to build compound boolean expressions. The remainder operator `rem`.

2 Assigning a name to an expression using the *name = expression* construct. Building compound expressions using **let** *name1 = expression1* **in let** *name2 = expression2* **in** ...

Functions, introduced by *name argument1 argument2 ... = expression*. These have type $a \rightarrow b$, $a \rightarrow b \rightarrow c$ etc. for some types a, b, c etc. Recursive functions. Turning a two-argument function into an operator with backticks like `rem`.

The types **Bool** and **Char**. The typeclasses **Num**, **Ord**, and **Eq**. A function from values of type a to type b with a in typeclass **Eq** and b in typeclass **Ord** would have type (**Eq** a, **Ord** b) $\Rightarrow$ a $\rightarrow$ b.

The special value it. The command :type and the use of Ctrl-C to interrupt a computation.

3 Matching patterns using f *pattern1 = expression1* ↩ f *pattern2 = expression2* etc... The expressions *expression1, expression2* etc. must have the same type as one another. Writing functions using guarded equations like f x | *guard = expression* ↩ | *guard2 = expression2* | **otherwise** ... The typeclass **Integral**.

4 Lists, which are ordered collections of zero or more elements of like type. They are written between square brackets, with elements separated by commas e.g. [1, 2, 3, 4, 5]. If a list is non-empty, it has a head, which is its first element, and a tail, which is the list composed of the rest of the elements.

The : "cons" operator, which adds an element to the front of a list. The ++ "append" operator, which concatenates two lists together.

Using the : "cons" symbol for pattern matching to distinguish lists of length zero, one, etc. and their contents.

The shorthand list syntax [1 .. 10] and [1, 3 .. 10]. The typeclass **Enum**. List comprehensions [*expression* | *name ← list, name2 ← list2, guard, guard2*].

Strings, which are sequences of characters written between double quotes and are of type [**Char**] or **String**.

5 The `div` operator. The use of **where** as an alternative to **let**.

6 Anonymous functions *name -> expression*. Making operators into functions as in (<) and (+). The . function composition operator. Defining new operators.

7 The **Maybe** type with its constructors Nothing and Just. The **Either** type with its constructors Left and Right. The **case** ... **of** ... construct.

8 Tuples to combine a fixed number of elements (x, y), (x, y, z) etc. with types (a, b), (a, b, c) etc.

9 Partial application of functions by giving fewer than the full number of arguments. Operator sections like (10 /).

10 New types with **data**. The **Show** typeclass. Implementing **Show** automatically with **deriving**. The show function to create strings from things of other types.

12 Typeclasses **Fractional**, **Floating** and **RealFrac**. The types **Integer**, **Int**, and **Double**. Built-in functions on values of these types such as sin, sqrt, and log. Conversion functions like fromIntegral and floor.

13 The potentially infinitely-long list [*expression* ..].

14 Input/output actions **IO**. The value ( ) of type ( ). Performing input/output actions with **do** and <- and **return**. Using **let** without **in** to introduce new names. The **Read** typeclass. FilePath, Handle and two sorts of IOMode: ReadMode and WriteMode. Importing a module with **import**.

15 The ghc command for compiling programs. Writing comments with --. Defining a module with **module** *name* **where**. Type abbreviations with **type**. Defining the main **IO** action with main. Getting command line arguments with getArgs.

16 Using the Standard Prelude and Base, and finding and reading their documentation.

Answers to Questions

Hints may be found on page 189.

Chapter 1 (Starting Off)

1

The expression 17 is a number and so is a value already. The expression 1 + 2 * 3 + 4 will evaluate to the value 11, since the multiplication has higher precedence than addition. The expression 400 > 200 evaluates to the boolean True since this is result of the comparison operator > on the operands 400 and 200. Similarly, 1 /= 1 evaluates to False. The expression True || False evaluates to True since one of the operands is true. Similarly, True && False evaluates to False since one of the operands is false. The expression **if** True **then** False **else** True evaluates to False since the first (**then**) part of the conditional expression is chosen, and takes the place of the entire expression. The expression '%' is a character and is already a value.

2

We need to put parentheses around the negative number -1 as described in the chapter text. The expression A == a was probably meant to be 'A' == 'a'. False and True need capital letters. An **if** ... **then** ... **else** ... construct must have an **else** ... part. The expression 'a' + 'b' gives an error because the + operator does not operate on characters.

3

The expression evaluates to 11. The programmer seems to be under the impression that spacing affects precedence. It does not, and so this use of space is misleading.

4

The \`rem\` operator is of higher precedence than the + operator. So 1 + 2 \`rem\` 3 and 1 + (2 \`rem\` 3) are the same expression, evaluating to 1 + 2 which is 3, but (1 + 2) \`rem\` 3 is the same as 3 \`rem\` 3, which is 0.

5

It prevents unexpected values: what would happen if a number other than 1 or 0 was calculated in the program – what would it mean? It is better just to use a different sort of value. We can then show more easily that a program is correct, since the number of possibilities has for the value has been reduced to just two.

6

The lowercase characters are in alphabetical order, for example 'p' < 'q' evaluates to True. The uppercase characters are similarly ordered. The uppercase letters are all "smaller" than the lowercase characters, so for example 'A' < 'a' evaluates to True. For booleans, False is considered "less than" True.

Chapter 2 (Names and Functions)

1

Just take in a number and return the number multiplied by ten. The function takes and returns a number, so the type is **Num** a ⇒ a → a.

```
GHCi:
Prelude> timesTen x = x * 10
Prelude> timesTen 7
70
```

x /= 0

chek if · is not · ample zero

2

We must take two arguments, and use the && and /= operators to test if they are both non-zero. So the result will be of type **Bool**. Each of the arguments must be a number, and must be able to be compared for equality with 0, so each must be of a type which is an instance of the typeclass **Num** and the typeclass **Eq**. It is not required that the two arguments are of the same type, though, since they are not operands to the same operator. The whole type will therefore be (**Eq** a, **Eq** b, **Num** a, **Num** b) ⇒ a → b → **Bool**.

```
GHCi:
Prelude> :{
Prelude| bothNonZero x y =
Prelude|    x /= 0 && y /= 0
Prelude| :}
Prelude> bothNonZero 10 (-1)
True
```

3

Our function should take a number and return another one (the sum). The base case is when the number is equal to 1. Then, the sum of all numbers from 1 . . . 1 is just 1. If not, we add the argument to the sum of all the numbers from 1 . . . (n − 1). Since the function must take a number which can be compared with 1, and return the same sort of number, it will have the type (**Eq** a, **Num** a) ⇒ a → a.

```
GHCi:
Prelude> :{
Prelude| sum' n =
Prelude|    if n == 1 then 1 else n + sum' (n - 1)
Prelude| :}
```

```
Prelude> sum' 10
55
```

The function is recursive. What happens if the number given is zero or negative?

4

A number to the power of 0 is 1. A number to the power of 1 is itself. Otherwise, the answer is the current n multiplied by n^{x-1}.

```
GHCi:
Prelude> :{
Prelude| power x n =
Prelude|   if n == 0 then 1 else (if n == 1 then x else x * power x (n - 1))
Prelude| :}
Prelude> power 2 5
32
```

Both arguments must be numbers. In addition, the second must be testable for equality. The result will have the same type as the first argument, so the type of power will be (**Eq** b, **Num** a, **Num** b) $\Rightarrow$ a $\rightarrow$ b $\rightarrow$ a. Notice that we had to put one **if** ... **then** ... **else** inside the **else** part of another to cope with the three different cases. The parentheses are not actually required, though, so we may write it like this:

```
GHCi:
Prelude> :{
Prelude| power x n =
Prelude|   if n == 0 then 1 else if n == 1 then x else x * power x (n - 1)
Prelude| :}
```

We could lay out the **if** ... **then** ... **else** ... construct over three lines like this:

```
power x n =
  if n == 0 then 1 else
  if n == 1 then x else
  x * power x (n - 1)
```

Or like this:

```
power x n =
  if n == 0 then 1
  else if n == 1 then x
  else x * power x (n - 1)
```

Which do you find easier to read? We can also remove the case for n == 1 since power x 1 will reduce to x * power x 0 which is just x.

5

The function `isConsonant` will have type **Char** → **Bool**. If a lower case character in the range `'a'`...`'z'` is not a vowel, it must be a consonant. So we can reuse the `isVowel` function we wrote earlier, and negate its result using the `not'` function:

```
GHCi:
Prelude> :{
Prelude| isVowel c =
Prelude|   c == 'a' || c == 'e' || c == 'i' || c == 'o' || c == 'u'
Prelude|
Prelude| isConsonant c =
Prelude|   not' (isVowel c)
Prelude| :}
Prelude> isConsonant 'x'
True
```

6

The expression is the same as **let** x = 1 **in** (**let** x = 2 **in** x + x), and so the result is 4. Both instances of x in x + x evaluate to 2 since this is the value assigned to the name x in the nearest enclosing **let** expression.

7

We could simply return 0 for a negative argument. The factorial of 0 is 1, so we can change that too, and say our new function finds the factorial of any non-negative number:

```
Prelude> :{
Prelude| factorial n =
Prelude|   if n < 0 then 0 else
Prelude|   if n == 0 then 1 else
Prelude|   n * factorial (n - 1)
Prelude| :}
Prelude> factorial 0
1
```

The number must be capable of being compared with 0 using equality and ordering. However, being an instance of typeclass **Ord** implies being an instance of typeclass **Eq**, so we need not mention **Eq** and the type is (**Num** a, **Ord** a) ⇒ a → a.

Later in the book, we will learn the proper way to deal with arguments for which there is no sensible answer.

8

1	**Num** a ⇒ a
1 + 2	**Num** a ⇒ a
f x y = x < y	**Ord** a ⇒ a → a → **Bool**
g x y = x < y + 2	(**Ord** a, **Num** a) ⇒ a → a → **Bool**
h x y = 0	**Num** a ⇒ b → c → a
i x y z = x + 10	**Num** a ⇒ a → b → c → a

9

46 * 10	::	**Num** a ⇒ a
2 > 1	::	**Bool**
f	::	**Num** a ⇒ a → a
g	::	(**Ord** a, **Num** a) ⇒ a → a → b → **Bool**
i	::	a → b → c → b

10

The expression `True + False` is not accepted because addition is not defined on booleans. Or, more formally, because the addition operator requires that its operands have a type which is an instance of the typeclass **Num**. The expression 6 + '6' is invalid for a similar reason. The character '6' and the number 6 are entirely unrelated. The function definition f x y z = (x < y) < (z + 1) is invalid because x < y has type **Bool** which cannot be compared with the expression z + 1.

11

The type **Num** a ⇒ b is not valid, since it tries to constrain a which is not mentioned to the right of the ⇒ symbol. The types **Num** a ⇒ a and **Num** t1 ⇒ t1 are equivalent, since a simple consistent renaming turns one into the other. The types **Num** a ⇒ a → b and **Num** b ⇒ b → a are similarly equivalent, though **Num** a ⇒ a → a is different.

The types (**Num** a, **Ord** a) ⇒ a → a and (**Ord** a, **Num** a) ⇒ a → a are equivalent: the order the typeclass constraints are given in is irrelevant.

12

Constraint **Eq** a is not required. All types in **Ord** are in **Eq**. So the examples read:

Ord a ⇒ a → b → a

(**Ord** a, **Eq** b) ⇒ b → b → a

Chapter 3 (Case by Case)

1

We can just pattern-match on the boolean. It does not matter, in this instance, which order the two cases are in.

```
not' :: Bool → Bool

not' True = False
not' False = True
```

2

Recall our solution from the previous chapter:

```
sum' :: (Eq a, Num a) ⇒ a → a

sum' n =
  if n == 1 then 1 else n + sum' (n - 1)
```

Modifying it to use pattern matching:

```
sumMatch :: (Eq a, Num a) ⇒ a → a

sumMatch 1 = 1
sumMatch n = n + sumMatch (n - 1)
```

Notice that the **Eq** typeclass appears even though we do not use the == operator. This is because the pattern-matching implicitly performs an equality test, to check if the argument is equal to one.

3

Again, modifying our solution from the previous chapter:

```
powerMatch :: (Num a, Num b, Eq b) ⇒ a → b → a

powerMatch _ 0 = 1
powerMatch x 1 = x
powerMatch x n = x * powerMatch x (n - 1)
```

4

We can write not' using guarded equations like this.

```
not' :: Bool → Bool

not' x | x == False = True
       | otherwise  = False
```

Or like this:

```
not' :: Bool → Bool

not' x | x          = False
       | otherwise  = True
```

Can you see why? Or, since we do not have to use **otherwise**, like this:

```
not' :: Bool → Bool

not' x | x == False = True
       | x == True  = False
```

The sumMatch rewrite is much the same:

```
sumMatch :: (Eq a, Num a) ⇒ a → a

sumMatch n | n == 1    = 1
           | otherwise = n + sumMatch (n - 1)
```

We can deduce that guarded equations are not really clearer when there are only two cases. The guarded equation version of powerMatch is much better:

```
powerMatch :: (Num a, Num b, Eq b) ⇒ a → b → a

powerMatch x n | n == 0    = 1
               | n == 1    = x
               | otherwise = x * powerMatch x (n - 1)
```

5

We need just three cases, remembering that characters may be compared using the comparison operators:

```
kind :: Num a ⇒ Char → a

kind c | c >= 'a' && c <= 'z' = 0
       | c >= 'A' && c <= 'Z' = 1
       | otherwise            = 2
```

Chapter 4 (Making Lists)

1

This is similar to oddElements:

```
evenElements :: [a] → [a]

evenElements [] = []                                      list has zero elements
evenElements [_] = []                              list has one element – drop it
evenElements (_:x:xs) = x : evenElements xs      keep second element, carry on
```

But we can perform the same trick as before, by reversing the cases, to reduce their number:

```
evenElements :: [a] → [a]

evenElements (_:x:xs) = x : evenElements xs       drop one, keep one, carry on
evenElements l = []                                otherwise, no more to drop
```

2

This is like counting the length of a list, but we only count if the current element is True.

```
countTrue :: Num a ⇒ [Bool] → a

countTrue [] = 0                                                       no more
countTrue (True:xs) = 1 + countTrue xs                          count this one
countTrue (False:xs) = countTrue xs                           but not this one
```

3

To make a palindrome from any list, we can append it to its reverse. To check if a list is a palindrome, we can compare it for equality with its reverse (the comparison operators work over almost all types).

```
makePalindrome :: [a] → [a]
isPalindrome :: Eq a ⇒ [a] → Bool

makePalindrome l =
  l ++ reverse' l

isPalindrome l =
  l == reverse' l
```

4

We pattern match with three cases. The empty list, where we have reached the last element, and where we have yet to reach it.

```
dropLast :: [a] → [a]

dropLast [] = []
dropLast [_] = []                              it is the last one, so remove it
dropLast (x:xs) = x : dropLast xs              at least two elements remain
```

5

The empty list cannot contain the element; if there is a non-empty list, either the head is equal to the element we are looking for, or if not, the result of our function is just the same as the result of recursing on the tail.

Note that we are using the property that || returns its right hand side if its left hand side is false to limit the recursion – our function really does stop as soon as it finds the element.

```
elem' :: Eq a ⇒ a → [a] → Bool

elem' e [] = False
elem' e (x:xs) = x == e || elem' e xs
```

6

If a list is empty, it is already a set. If not, either the head exists somewhere in the tail or it does not; if it does exist in the tail, we can discard it, since it will be included later. If not, we must include it.

```
makeSet :: Eq a ⇒ [a] → [a]

makeSet [] = []
makeSet (x:xs) = if elem' x xs then makeSet xs else x : makeSet xs
```

For example, consider the evaluation of makeSet [4, 5, 6, 5, 4]:

$$
\begin{array}{ll}
 & \text{makeSet } [4, 5, 6, 5, 4] \\
\Longrightarrow & \text{makeSet } [5, 6, 5, 4] \\
\Longrightarrow & \text{makeSet } [6, 5, 4] \\
\Longrightarrow & 6 : \text{makeSet } [5, 4] \\
\Longrightarrow & 6 : 5 : \text{makeSet } [4] \\
\Longrightarrow & 6 : 5 : 4 : \text{makeSet } [] \\
\Longrightarrow & 6 : 5 : 4 : [] \\
\overset{*}{\Longrightarrow} & [6, 5, 4]
\end{array}
$$

7

The first part of the evaluation of reverse' takes time proportional to the length of the list, processing each element once. However, when the lists are appended together, the order of the operations is such that the first argument becomes longer each time. The ++ operator, as we know, also takes time proportional to the length of its first argument. And so, this accumulating of the lists takes time proportional to the square of the length of the list.

$$
\begin{array}{ll}
& \text{reverse' [1, 2, 3, 4]} \\
\Longrightarrow & \text{reverse' [2, 3, 4] ++ [1]} \\
\Longrightarrow & \text{(reverse' [3, 4] ++ [2]) ++ [1]} \\
\Longrightarrow & \text{((reverse' [4] ++ [3]) ++ [2]) ++ [1]} \\
\Longrightarrow & \text{(((reverse' [] ++ [4]) ++ [3]) ++ [2]) ++ [1]} \\
\Longrightarrow & \text{(((([] ++ [4]) ++ [3]) ++ [2]) ++ [1]} \\
\Longrightarrow & \text{(([4] ++ [3]) ++ [2]) ++ [1]} \\
\Longrightarrow & \text{([4, 3] ++ [2]) ++ [1]} \\
\Longrightarrow & \text{[4, 3, 2] ++ [1]} \\
\Longrightarrow & \text{[4, 3, 2, 1]}
\end{array}
$$

By using an additional argument to collect results – called an *accumulator,* we can write a version which operates in time proportional to the length of the list:

```
revInner :: [a] → [a] → [a]
reverse' :: [a] → [a]

revInner a [] = a
revInner a (x:xs) = revInner (x : a) xs

reverse' l =
  revInner [] l
```

For the same list:

$$
\begin{array}{ll}
& \text{reverse' [1, 2, 3, 4]} \\
\Longrightarrow & \text{revInner [] [1, 2, 3, 4]} \\
\Longrightarrow & \text{revInner (1 : []) [2, 3, 4]} \\
\Longrightarrow & \text{revInner (2 : 1 : []) [3, 4]} \\
\Longrightarrow & \text{revInner (3 : 2 : 1 : []) [4]} \\
\Longrightarrow & \text{revInner (4 : 3 : 2 : 1 : []) []} \\
\Longrightarrow & \text{4 : 3 : 2 : 1 : []} \\
= & \text{[4, 3, 2, 1]}
\end{array}
$$

8

Both are [ ]. We can use the reverse' function already defined, and write reverse' [1 .. 10]. In fact, we may also write [10,9 .. 1].

9

We can use a guard:

```
GHCi:
Prelude> [x | x <- [1 .. 9999], x `rem` 21 == 0 && x `rem` 83 == 0]
[1743,3486,5229,6972,8715]
Prelude> [x | x <- [1 .. 9999], x `rem` 21 == 0 || x `rem` 83 == 0]
[21,42,63,83,84,105,126,147,166,168,189,210,231,249,252,273,294......
```

Instead of the && operator, for the first case, we can use two guards:

```
GHCi:
Prelude> [x | x <- [1 .. 9999], x `rem` 21 == 0, x `rem` 83 == 0]
[1743,3486,5229,6972,8715]
```

10

We can generate the list of just the True entries and then count the length, writing:

```
GHCi:
Prelude> countTrue l = length' [x | x <- l, x == True]
Prelude> countTrue [True, False, True]
2
```

But, of course, x == True is just the same as x, since x is a boolean. So we may simplify:

```
GHCi:
Prelude> countTrue l = length' [x | x <- l, x]
Prelude> countTrue [True, False, True]
2
```

Chapter 5 (Sorting Things)

1

We may rewrite with the **where** construct. Notice that the name n is defined in the first line of the **where** construct and used in the second and third lines.

```
mergeSort :: Ord a ⇒ [a] → [a]

mergeSort [] = []                                   we are done if the list is empty
mergeSort [x] = [x]                                and also if it only has one element
mergeSort l =
  merge (mergeSort left) (mergeSort right)                    sort and merge them
    where
      n = length' l `div` 2
      left = take' n l                                       get the left hand half
      right = drop' n l                                     and the right hand half
```

Alternatively, using **let** to define a name representing the number we will take or drop:

```
mergeSort :: Ord a ⇒ [a] → [a]

mergeSort [] = []                                    we are done if the list is empty
mergeSort [x] = [x]                            and also if it only has one element
mergeSort l =
  let n = length' l `div` 2 in
    let left = take' n l                                get the left hand half
        right = drop' n l                             and the right hand half
    in
        merge (mergeSort left) (mergeSort right)        sort and merge them
```

2

The argument to take' or drop' is length' l `div` 2 which is clearly less than or equal to length' l for all possible values of l. Thus, take' and drop' always succeed. In our case, take' and drop' are only called when length' l is more than 1, due to the pattern matching.

3

We may simply replace the <= operator with the >= operator in the insert function.

```
insert :: Ord a ⇒ a → [a] → [a]

insert x [] = [x]
insert x (y:ys) =
  if x >= y
    then x : y : ys
    else y : insert x ys
```

The sort function is unaltered.

4

We require a function of type [a] → **Bool**. List of length zero and one are, by definition, sorted. If the list is longer, check that its first two elements are in sorted order. If this is true, also check that the rest of the list is sorted, starting with the second element.

```
isSorted :: Ord a ⇒ [a] → Bool

isSorted [] = True
isSorted [x] = True
isSorted (x:x':xs) = x <= x' && isSorted (x' : xs)
```

We can reverse the cases to simplify:

```
isSorted :: Ord a ⇒ [a] → Bool

isSorted (x:x':t) = x <= x' && isSorted (x' : xs)
isSorted _ = True
```

5

Lists are compared starting with their first elements. If the elements differ, they are compared, and that is the result of the comparison. If both have the same first element, the second elements are considered, and so on. If the end of one list is reached before the other, the shorter list is considered smaller. For example:

[1] < [1,2] < [2] < [2, 1] < [2, 2]

These are the same principles you use to look up a word in a dictionary: compare the first letters – if same, compare the second etc. So, when applied to the example in the question, it has the effect of sorting the words into alphabetical order.

6

First, using **where**:

```
sortComplete :: Ord a ⇒ [a] → [a]

sortComplete [] = []
sortComplete (x:xs) = insert x (sortComplete xs)
  where
    insert a [] = [a]
    insert a (x:xs) =
      if a <= x then a : x : xs else x : insert a xs
```

Now using the **let** … **in** … construct:

```
sortComplete :: Ord a ⇒ [a] → [a]

sortComplete [] = []
sortComplete (x:xs) =
  let insert a [] = [a]
      insert a (x:xs) =
        if a <= x then a : x : xs else x : insert a xs
  in
    insert x (sortComplete xs)
```

Chapter 6 (Functions upon Functions upon Functions)

1

Our function will have type **String** → **String**. We just match on the argument character list: if it is empty, we are done. If it starts with an exclamation mark, we output a period, and carry on. If not, we output the character unchanged, and carry on:

```
calm :: String → String

calm [] = []
calm ('!':xs) = '.' : calm xs
calm (x:xs) = x : calm xs
```

To use map' instead, we write a simple function calmChar to process a single character. We can then use map' to build our main function:

```
calmChar :: Char → Char
calm :: String → String

calmChar '!' = '.'
calmChar x = x

calm l =
  map' calmChar l
```

This avoids the explicit recursion of the original, and so it is easier to see what is going on.

2

The clip function is of type (**Num** a, **Ord** a) ⇒ a → a and is easy to write:

```
clip :: (Num a, Ord a) ⇒ a → a

clip x =
  if x < 1 then 1 else
    if x > 10 then 10 else x
```

Now we can use map' for the clipList function:

```
clipList :: (Num a, Ord a) ⇒ [a] → [a]

clipList l =
  map' clip l
```

We can write the `clip` function more neatly with guarded equations:

```
clip :: (Num a, Ord a) ⇒ a → a

clip x | x < 1 = 1
       | x > 10 = 10
       | otherwise = x
```

3

Just put the body of the clip function inside an anonymous function:

```
clipList :: (Num a, Ord a) ⇒ [a] → [a]

clipList l =
  map'
    (\x ->
      if x < 1 then 1 else
        if x > 10 then 10 else x)
    l
```

4

We require a function `apply f n x` which applies function `f` a total of `n` times to the initial value `x`. The base case is when `n` is zero.

```
apply :: (Eq b, Num b) ⇒ (a → a) → b → a → a

apply f 0 x = x                          just x
apply f n x = f (apply f (n - 1) x)      reduce problem size by one
```

Consider the type:

$$\text{(Eq b, Num b)} \Rightarrow \overbrace{(a \to a)}^{\text{function f}} \to \overbrace{b}^{n} \to \overbrace{a}^{x} \to \overbrace{a}^{\text{result}}$$

The function `f` must take and return the same type, since its result in one iteration is fed back in as its argument in the next. Therefore, the argument `x` and the final result must also have a suitable type, but must be in typeclass **Eq** (for the comparison with 0) and typeclass **Num** (for the subtraction of 1). For example, we might have a power function:

```
power :: (Eq b, Num b, Num a) ⇒ a → b → a

power a b =
  apply (\x -> x * a) b 1
```

So power a b calculates a^b. The extra constraint **Num** b comes from the $*$ operator used inside the function passed to apply.

5

We can add an extra argument to the insert function, and use that instead of the comparison operator:

```
insert :: (a → a → Bool) → a → [a] → [a]

insert f x [] = [x]                              add extra argument f
insert f x (y:ys) =
  if f x y
    then x : y : ys
    else y : insert f x ys                       remember to add f here too
```

Now we just need to rewrite the sort function.

```
sort :: (a → a → Bool) → [a] → [a]

sort f [] = []
sort f (x:xs) = insert f x (sort f xs)
```

6

We cannot use map' here, because the result list will not necessarily be the same length as the argument list. The function will have type (a → **Bool**) → [a] → [a].

```
filter' :: (a → Bool) → [a] → [a]

filter' f [] = []
filter' f (x:xs) =
  if f x
    then x : filter' f xs
    else filter' f xs
```

For example, filter' (\x -> x `rem` 2 == 0) [1, 2, 4, 5] evaluates to [2, 4].

7

The function will have type (a → **Bool**) → [a] → **Bool**.

```
all' :: (a → Bool) → [a] → Bool

all' f [] = True
all' f (x:xs) = f x && all' f xs                 true for this one, and all the others
```

For example, we can see if all elements of a list are positive: `all' (\x -> x > 0) [1, 2, -1]` evaluates to `False`. Notice that we are relying on the fact that `&&` only evaluates its right hand side when the left hand side is true to limit the recursion.

8

The function will have type $(a \rightarrow b) \rightarrow [[a]] \rightarrow [[b]]$. We use `map'` on each element of the list.

```
mapl :: (a → b) → [[a]] → [[b]]

mapl f [] = []
mapl f (x:xs) = map' f x : mapl f xs
```

We have used explicit recursion to handle the outer list, and `map'` to handle each inner list.

9

Without the composition operator, we may use the filter function from Question 6, and write:

```
GHCi:
Prelude> f l = reverse' (sort (<) (filter' (\x -> x `rem` 15 == 0) l))
Prelude> f [1 .. 100]
[90,75,60,45,30,15]
```

Now, we can use the composition operator instead:

```
GHCi:
Prelude> f = reverse' . sort (<) . filter' (\x -> x `rem` 15 == 0)
Prelude> f [1 .. 100]
[90,75,60,45,30,15]
```

Note that we have to drop the argument `l` for this to work.

Chapter 7 (When Things Go Wrong)

1

The function `s`, used by `smallest` works through the input list one item at a time, keeping track of the smallest number found so far, and updating it if necessary. When the input list is empty, the smallest element (if any) is returned.

```
smallest :: (Num a, Ord a) ⇒ [a] → Maybe a

smallest x = s Nothing x where
  s Nothing [] = Nothing
  s (Just a) [] = Just a
  s Nothing (x:xs) =
    if x > 0
      then s (Just x) xs
      else s Nothing xs
  s (Just a) (x:xs) =
    if x > 0 && x < a
      then s (Just x) xs
      else s (Just a) xs
```

2

We just surround the call to smallest.

```
smallest0 :: (Num a, Ord a) ⇒ [a] → a

smallest0 l =
  case smallest l of
    Nothing -> 0
    Just a -> a
```

3

We write a function s which, given a test number x and a target number n squares x and tests if it is more than n. If it is, the answer is x - 1. The test number will be initialized at 1. The function sqrtMaybe returns Nothing if the number is negative and otherwise begins the testing process.

```
sqrtMaybe :: (Num a, Ord a) ⇒ a → Maybe a

sqrtMaybe n =
  if n < 0 then Nothing else Just (s 1 n)
    where
      s x n = if x * x > n then x - 1 else s (x + 1) n
```

4

This is a simple variation on mapMaybe. We test the result of applying the function to each element, substituting the default value when Nothing is returned.

```
mapMaybeDefault :: (a → Maybe b) → b → [a] → [b]

mapMaybeDefault f _ [] = []
mapMaybeDefault f d (x:xs) =
  case f x of
    Just r -> r : mapMaybeDefault f d xs
    Nothing -> d : mapMaybeDefault f d xs
```

5

We use **let** to assign names to the parts of the tuple returned by processing the rest of the list, then apply the function to the first element, building the new result tuple.

```
splitEither :: (a → Either b c) → [a] → ([b], [c])

splitEither f [] = ([], [])
splitEither f (x:xs) =
  let (ls, rs) = splitEither f xs in
    case f x of
      Left l -> (l : ls, rs)
      Right r -> (ls, r : rs)
```

Chapter 8 (Looking Things Up)

1

Since the keys must be unique, the number of different keys is simply the length of the list representing the dictionary – so we can just use the usual length' function.

2

The type is the same as for the add function, but with a **Maybe** in the return type. However, if we reach the end of the list, we return Nothing, since we did not manage to find the entry to replace.

```
replace :: Eq a ⇒ a → b → [(a, b)] → Maybe [(a, b)]

replace k v [] = Nothing                              could not find it
replace k v ((k', v'):xs) =
  if k == k' then Just ((k, v) : xs) else             found it – replace
    case replace k v t of
      Just xs' -> Just ((k', v') : xs')        already found and replaced
      Nothing -> Nothing                                     not found
```

3

The function takes a list of keys and a list of values and returns a dictionary if it succeeds. So it will have type [a] → [b] → **Maybe** [(a, b)].

```
makeDict :: [a] → [b] → Maybe [(a, b)]

makeDict [] [] = Just []
makeDict _ [] = Nothing
makeDict [] _ = Nothing
makeDict (k:ks) (v:vs) =
  case makeDict ks vs of
    Nothing -> Nothing
    Just xs -> Just ((k, v) : xs)
```

4

This will have the type [(a, b)] → ([a], [b]). For the first time, we need to return a pair, building up both result lists element by element. This is rather awkward, since we will need the tails of both of the eventual results, so we can attach the new heads.

```
makeLists :: [(a, b)] → ([a], [b])

makeLists [] = ([], [])                        build the empty pair
makeLists ((k, v):xs) = (k : ks, v : vs)   there is at least one key-value pair
  where (ks, vs) = makeLists xs
```

We do this by using the **where** construct to do what is effectively pattern matching on one pattern, allowing it to assign the names ks and vs simultaneously.

Here is a sample evaluation (we cannot really show it in the conventional way, so you must work through it whilst looking at the function definition):

$$
\begin{aligned}
&\quad\quad\text{makeLists } [(1, 2), (3, 4), (5, 6)] \\
\implies&\quad\quad\quad\quad\text{makeLists } [(3, 4), (5, 6)] \\
\implies&\quad\quad\quad\quad\quad\quad\text{makeLists } [(5, 6)] \\
\implies&\quad\quad\quad\quad\quad\quad\quad\quad\text{makeLists } [] \\
\implies&\quad\quad\quad\quad\quad\quad\quad\quad\quad\quad ([], []) \\
\implies&\quad\quad\quad\quad\quad\quad\quad\quad\quad ([5], [6]) \\
\implies&\quad\quad\quad\quad\quad\quad\quad ([3, 5], [4, 6]) \\
\implies&\quad\quad\quad\quad\quad ([1, 3, 5], [2, 4, 6])
\end{aligned}
$$

5

We can use our `elem'` function which determines whether an element is a member of a list, building up a list of the keys we have already seen, and adding to the result list of key-value pairs only those with new keys.

```
dictionaryOfPairsInner :: Eq a ⇒ [a] → [(a, b)] → [(a, b)]
dictionaryOfPairs :: Eq a ⇒ [(a, b)] → [(a, b)]

dictionaryOfPairsInner keysSeen [] = []
dictionaryOfPairsInner keysSeen ((k, v):xs) =
  if elem' k keysSeen
    then dictionaryOfPairsInner keysSeen xs
    else (k, v) : dictionaryOfPairsInner (k : keysSeen) xs

dictionaryOfPairs l =
  dictionaryOfPairsInner [] l
```

How long does this take to run? Consider how long `elem'` takes.

6

We pattern match on the first list – if it is empty, the result is simply the second list. Otherwise, we add the first element of the first list to the union of the rest of its elements and the second list.

```
union :: Eq a ⇒ [(a, b)] → [(a, b)] → [(a, b)]

union [] ys = ys
union ((k, v):xs) ys = add k v (union xs ys)
```

We can verify that the elements of the first dictionary have precedence over the elements of the second dictionary by noting that add replaces a value if the key already exists.

Chapter 9 (More with Functions)

1

The function g a b c has type a → b → c → d which can also be written a → (b → (c → d)). Thus, it takes an argument of type a and returns a function of type b → (c → d) which, when you give it an argument of type b returns a function of type c → d which, when you give it an argument of type c returns something of type d. And so, we can apply just one or two arguments to the function g (which is called partial application), or apply all three at once. When we write g a b c = ... this is just shorthand for g = \a -> \b -> \c -> ...

2

The type of elem' is **Eq** a ⇒ a → [a] → **Bool**, so if we partially apply the first argument, the type of elem' e must be **Eq** a ⇒ [a] → **Bool**. We can use the partially-applied elem' function and map' to produce a list of boolean values, one for each list in the argument, indicating whether or not that list contains the element. Then, we can use elem' again to make sure there are no False booleans in the list.

```
elemAll :: Eq a ⇒ a → [[a]] → Bool

elemAll e ls =
  let booleans = map' (elem' e) ls in
    not' (elem' False booleans)
```

We could also write:

```
elemAll :: Eq a ⇒ a → [[a]] → Bool

elemAll e ls =
  not' (elem' False (map' (elem' e) ls))
```

Here it is using the . operator:

```
elemAll :: Eq a ⇒ a → [[a]] → Bool

elemAll e =
  not' . (elem' False) . (map' (elem' e))
```

Which do you think is clearer? Why do we check for the absence of False rather than the presence of True?

3

The function map' has type (a → b) → [a] → [b]. The function mapl we wrote has type (a → b) → [[a]] → [[b]]. So the function mapll will have type (a → b) → [[[a]]] → [[[b]]]. It may be defined thus:

```
mapll :: (a → b) → [[[a]]] → [[[b]]]

mapll f l = map' (map' (map' f)) l
```

But, as discussed, we may remove the ls too:

```
mapll :: (a → b) → [[[a]]] → [[[b]]]

mapll f = map' (map' (map' f))
```

In fact, making use of the . operator gives the simplest and neatest form:

```
mapll :: (a → b) → [[[a]]] → [[[b]]]

mapll = map' . map' . map'
```

4

We can write a function to truncate a single list using our take' function, being careful to deal with the case where there is not enough to take, and then use this and map' to build truncateLists itself.

```
truncateList :: (Ord a, Num a) ⇒ a → [b] → [b]
truncateLists :: (Ord a, Num a) ⇒ a → [[b]] → [[b]]

truncateList n l =
  if length' l >= n then take' n l else l

truncateLists n ll = map' (truncateList n) ll
```

Here we have used partial application of truncateList to build a suitable function for map'.

5

First, define a function which takes the given number and a list, returning the first element (or the number if none). We can then build the main function, using partial application to make a suitable function to give to map':

```
firstElt :: a → [a] → a
firstElts :: a → [[a]] → [a]

firstElt n [] = n
firstElt n (x:_) = x

firstElts n l = map' (firstElt n) l
```

6

We can use map' and an operator section, and write:

```
GHCi:
Prelude> addNum n ls = map' (n :) ls
Prelude> addNum 1 [[2], [3, 4]]
[[1,2],[1,3,4]]
```

Chapter 10 (New Kinds of Data)

1

We need two constructors – one for squares, which needs just a single number (the length of a side), and one for rectangles which needs two numbers (the width and height, in that order):

```
data Rect a = Square a
            | Rectangle a a deriving Show
```

The name of our new type is Rect. A Rect is either a Square or a Rectangle. Just like the Colour type in the chapter text, the type variable a is used to stand for the type of the data accompanying the constructors. In our scenario, it will always be a number. For example,

```
s :: Num a ⇒ Rect a
r :: Num a ⇒ Rect a

s = Square 7

r = Rectangle 5 2                                    width 5, height 2
```

2

We pattern match on the argument:

```
area :: Num a ⇒ Rect a → a

area (Square s) = s * s
area (Rectangle w h) = w * h
```

3

This will be a function of type Rect a → Rect a. Squares remain unaltered, but if we have a rectangle with a bigger width than height, we rotate it by ninety degrees.

```
rotate :: Ord a ⇒ Rect a → Rect a

rotate (Rectangle w h) =
  if w > h then Rectangle h w else Rectangle w h
rotate (Square s) = Square s
```

4

We will use `map'` to perform our rotation on any Rects in the argument list which need it. We will then use the sorting function from the previous chapter which takes a custom comparison function so as to just compare the widths.

```
widthOfRect :: Rect a → a
rectCompare :: Ord a ⇒ Rect a → Rect → Bool
pack :: Ord a ⇒ [Rect a] → [Rect a]

widthOfRect (Square s) = s
widthOfRect (Rectangle w _) = w

rectCompare a b =
  widthOfRect a < widthOfRect b

pack rs =
  sort rectCompare (map' rotate rs)
```

For example, packing the list of rects

```
[Square 6, Rectangle 4 3, Rectangle 5 6, Square 2]
```

will give

```
[Square 2, Rectangle 3 4, Rectangle 5 6, Square 6]
```

5

We follow the same pattern as for lists, being careful to deal with exceptional circumstances:

```
seqTake :: (Eq a, Num a) ⇒ a → Sequence b → Maybe (Sequence a)
seqDrop :: (Eq a, Num a) ⇒ a → Sequence b → Maybe (Sequence a)
seqMap :: (a → b) → Sequence a → Sequence b

seqTake 0 _ = Just Nil
seqTake _ Nil = Nothing
seqTake n (Cons x xs) =
  case seqTake (n - 1) xs of
    Nothing -> Nothing
    Just xs' -> Just (Cons x xs')

seqDrop 0 xs = Just xs
seqDrop _ Nil = Nothing
seqDrop n (Cons _ xs) = seqDrop (n - 1) xs

seqMap _ Nil = Nil
seqMap f (Cons x xs) = Cons (f x) (seqMap f xs)
```

6

We can use our power function from Chapter 2 Question 4:

```
evaluate :: Expr a → a

data Expr a = Num a
            | Add Expr Expr
            | Subtract Expr Expr
            | Multiply Expr Expr
            | Divide Expr Expr
            | Power Expr Expr deriving Show

evaluate (Num x) = x
evaluate (Add e e') = evaluate e + evaluate e'
evaluate (Multiply e e') = evaluate e - evaluate e'
evaluate (Divide e e') = evaluate e `div` evaluate e'
evaluate (Power e e') = power (evaluate e) (evaluate e')
```

Chapter 11 (Growing Trees)

1

Our function will have type **Eq** a ⇒ a → Tree a → **Bool**. It takes a element to look for, a tree holding that sort of element, and returns True if the element is found, or False otherwise.

```
treeMember :: Eq a ⇒ a → Tree a → Bool

treeMember x Lf = False
treeMember x (Br y l r) =
  x == y || treeMember x l || treeMember x r
```

Note that we have placed the test x == y first of the three to ensure earliest termination upon finding an appropriate element.

2

Our function will have type Tree a → Tree a. A leaf flips to a leaf. A branch has its left and right swapped, and we must recursively flip its left and right sub-trees too.

```
treeFlip :: Tree a → Tree a

treeFlip Lf = Lf
treeFlip (Br x l r) = Br x (treeFlip r) (treeFlip l)
```

3

We can check each part of both trees together. Leaves are considered equal, branches are equal if their left and right sub-trees are equal.

```
equalShape :: Tree a → Tree b → Bool

equalShape Lf Lf = True
equalShape (Br _ l r) (Br _ l2 r2) =
  equalShape l l2 && equalShape r r2
equalShape _ _ = False
```

4

We can use the tree insertion operation repeatedly:

```
treeOfList :: Ord a ⇒ [(a, b)] → Tree (a, b)

treeOfList [] = Lf
treeOfList ((k, v):xs) = treeInsert (treeOfList xs) k v
```

There will be no key clashes, because the argument should already be a dictionary. If it is not, earlier keys are preferred since `treeInsert` replaces existing keys.

5

We can make list dictionaries from both tree dictionaries, append them, and build a new tree from the resultant list.

```
treeUnion :: Ord a ⇒ Tree (a, b) → Tree (a, b) → Tree (a, b)

treeUnion t t' =
  treeOfList (listOfTree t ++ listOfTree t')
```

The combined list may not be a dictionary (because it may have repeated keys), but `treeOfList` will prefer keys encountered earlier. So, we put entries from t' after those from t.

6

We will use a list for the sub-trees of each branch, with the empty list signifying there are no more i.e. that this is the bottom of the tree. Thus, we only need a single constructor.

```
data Mtree a = Branch a [Mtree a] deriving Show
```

So, now we can define `size`, `total`, and `map` functions:

```
mTreeSize :: Num a ⇒ Mtree b → a
mTreeTotal :: Num a ⇒ Mtree a → a
mTreeMap :: (b → a) → Mtree b → Mtree a

mTreeSize (Branch _ l) = 1 + sum' (map' mTreeSize l)

mTreeTotal (Branch e l) = e + sum' (map' mTreeTotal l)

mTreeMap f (Branch e l) = Branch (f e) (map' (mTreeMap f) l)
```

Chapter 12 (The Other Numbers)

1

We represent points as pairs (2-tuples) of numbers. Since we use /, **Fractional** appears in the type.

```
between :: (Fractional a, Fractional b) ⇒ (a, b) → (a, b) → (a, b)

between (x, y) (x', y') =
  ((x + x') / 2, (y + y') / 2)
```

Note, however, that the x-coordinate need not have the same type as the y-coordinate, so long as they are both instances of **Fractional**. Normally, of course, we would expect a and b to be the same type.

2

The `ceiling` function has type (**RealFrac** a, **Integral** b) ⇒ a → b just like `floor`. We test to see which of the two our number is closest to:

```
roundNum :: (RealFrac a, Integral b) ⇒ a → b

roundNum x =
  if fromIntegral c - x <= x - fromIntegral f then c else f
    where c = ceiling x
          f = floor x
```

We use `fromIntegral` to make sure we can use the real subtraction operator to calculate which number is nearest. We could use `floor (x + 0.5)` instead of `ceiling` if we liked.

Note that it is not quite obvious how rounding should work, with respect to negative numbers, and with respect to numbers which are exactly halfway between integers, such as 3.5. What rules does our `roundNum` obey? What rules does the built-in Haskell function `round` obey?

3

The whole part is calculated using the built-in `floor` function. We return a tuple, the first number being the whole part, the second being the original number minus the whole part. In the case of a negative number, we must be careful – `floor` always rounds downward, not toward zero!

```
parts :: RealFrac a ⇒ a → (Integer, a)

parts x =
  if x < 0 then
    let (a, b) = parts (- x) in
      (- a, b)
  else
    (floor x, x - fromIntegral (floor x))
```

Notice that we are using the unary negation operator - to make the number positive. We use `fromIntegral` to convert the result of the `floor` function into a number of an appropriate type.

4

First we write a function `makeLine` which, given a position, creates a line of spaces, an asterisk, and a newline character:

```
replicate' :: (Eq a, Num a) ⇒ a → b → [b]
makeLine :: (Num a, Eq a) ⇒ a → String

replicate' 0 _ = []
replicate' n x = x : replicate' (n - 1) x

makeLine x =
  replicate' x ' ' ++ ['*', '\n']
```

It uses the function `replicate'` which makes a list containing many copies of a value. Now we need to determine at which column the asterisk will be printed. It is important to make sure that the range $0 \ldots 1$ is split into fifty equal sized parts, which requires some careful thought. Then, we just print enough spaces to pad the line, add the asterisk, and a newline character.

```
star :: RealFrac a ⇒ a → String

star x =
  let i = floor (x * 50) in
    let i' = if i == 50 then 49 else i in
      makeLine (if i' == 0 then 0 else i' - 1)
```

5

We concatenate the results of all the calls to star, which results in the graph:

```
plot :: (Ord a, Num a, RealFrac b) ⇒ (a → b) → a → a → a → String

plot f a b dy =
  if a > b then
    []
  else
    star (f a) ++ plot f (a + dy) b dy
```

No allowance has been made here for bad arguments (for example, b smaller than a). Can you extend our program to move the zero-point to the middle of the screen, so that the sine function can be graphed even when its result is less than zero?

6

The types **Bool** and **Char** may be compared for equality and ordered, but they cannot provide the operations necessary to fit into any of the numeric typeclasses. They can, however be enumerated (try [False ..] or ['a' .. 'z']). So we may update the diagram:

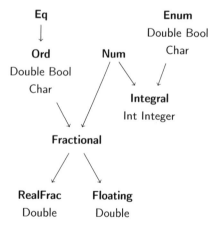

Chapter 13 (Being Lazy)

1

This is similar to the from function in the text, but we double every time instead of adding one.

```
doubleFrom :: Num a ⇒ a → [a]
doubles :: Num a ⇒ [a]

doubleFrom n = n : doubleFrom (n * 2)

doubles = doubleFrom 1
```

Having written the function which, given a number, doubles from that point, we then just code the list itself by starting at 1. We could use the **where** construct to code the list in one shot:

```
doubles :: Num a ⇒ [a]

doubles = doubleFrom 1 where
  doubleFrom n = n : doubleFrom (n * 2)
```

2

This is as simple as using the ++ operator:

```
repeating :: [a] → [a]

repeating l = l ++ repeating l
```

What happens with repeating []?

3

The first two Fibonacci numbers are defined to be 0 and 1, so we must give them explicitly. The inner function then puts the first number at the head of the list and shifts everything along one place.

```
fibInner :: Num a ⇒ a → a → [a]
fib :: Num a ⇒ [a]

fibInner x y = x : fibInner y (x + y)

fib = fibInner 0 1
```

Since we are unlikely to need to use fibInner outside of fib, we can rewrite with the **where** constuct:

```
fib :: Num a ⇒ [a]

fib = fibInner 0 1 where
  fibInner x y = x : fibInner y (x + y)
```

4

We can use a tree type with no `Lf` constructor, since our tree will always be infinitely large:

```
data Tree a = Br a (Tree a) (Tree a)
```

We do not use **deriving** Show because its printed representation will always be infinite. Recall our list version:

```
allFrom :: Num a ⇒ [a] → Tree [a]
allLists :: Num a ⇒ Tree [a]

allFrom l =
  Br l (allFrom (0 : l)) (allFrom (1 : l))

allLists = allFrom []
```

In a similar fashion, we can define one for our new tree type, making use of `interleave` to be sure the left- and right-hand parts of each branch are dealt with fairly:

```
makeList :: Tree a → [a]

makeList (Br x l r) = x : interleave (makeList l) (makeList r)
```

5

We must start with the longest pattern, to avoid any list matching with `x:xs` rather then `x:x':xs`.

```
unleave :: [a] → ([a], [a])

unleave (x : x' : xs) =
  (x : ys, x' : zs) where (ys, zs) = unleave xs
unleave (x : _) = ([x], [])
unleave [] = ([], [])
```

Chapter 14 (In and Out)

1

We can write a helper function `printIntegersInner` which prints the numbers and the commas, being careful to give special attention to the last one in the list. Then, the main function `printIntegers` puts the square brackets on.

```
printIntegersInner :: Show a ⇒ [a] → IO ()
printIntegers :: Show a ⇒ [a] → IO ()

printIntegersInner [] = return ()
printIntegersInner [x] =
  putStr (show x)
printIntegersInner (x:xs) =
  do putStr (show x)
     putStr ","
     printIntegersInner xs

printIntegers l =
  do putStr "["
     printIntegersInner l
     putStr "]"
```

But we notice, from the type, that our function can actually print a list of any showable thing. So its name is somewhat misleading.

2

Our readThree IO action results in three integers from the user's input. So it has type IO (Integer, Integer, Integer). We use the do and <- constructs together with getIntegerMaybe to ask for the three integers in turn, then check that they were valid.

```
readThree :: IO (Integer, Integer, Integer)

readThree =
  do x <- getIntegerMaybe
     y <- getIntegerMaybe
     z <- getIntegerMaybe
     case (x, y, z) of
       (Just a, Just b, Just c) -> return (a, b, c)
       _ ->
         do putStrLn "Not valid integers. Please try again"
            readThree
```

Alternatively, one might read and check each integer individually.

3

Again, we use getIntegerMaybe. This time to write a function readDictNumber which builds an IO action which reads a given number of dictionary entries, making sure to deal with user mistakes. The IO action readDict deals with asking the user how many entries will be input, again detecting user mistakes.

```
readDictNumber :: Integer → IO [(Integer, String)]
readDict :: IO [(Integer, String)]

readDictNumber n =
  if n == 0 then return [] else
    do i <- getIntegerMaybe
       name <- getLine
       case i of
         Nothing ->
           do putStrLn "Not a valid integer."
              readDictNumber n
         Just x ->
           do rest <- readDictNumber (n - 1)
              return ((x, name) : rest)

readDict =
  do putStrLn "How many dictionary entries to input?"
     n <- getIntegerMaybe
     case n of
       Nothing ->
         do putStrLn "Not a number."
            readDict
       Just i ->
         if i < 0 then
           do putStrLn "Number is negative."
              readDict
         else
           readDictNumber i
```

4

We build a function row which, given a file handle and a list of numbers, builds an **IO** action to print out that list separated by spaces. Now, the function rows builds a compound **IO** action to print such a list of numbers, multiplied by a given multiplier n, using row and move to the next line. The main function table deals with the tasks of opening and closing the file, and printing out the rows, using multipliers from 1 to n.

```
row  :: Handle → [Integer] → IO ()
rows :: Handle → Integer → [Integer] → IO ()
table :: FilePath → Integer → IO ()

row fh [] = return ()
row fh (x:xs) =
  do hPutStr fh (show x)
     hPutStr fh "\xs"
     row fh xs

rows fh n [] = return ()
rows fh n (x:xs) =
  do row fh (map (* x) [1 .. n])
     hPutStr fh "\n"
     rows fh n xs

table filename n =
  do fh <- openFile filename WriteMode
     rows fh n [1 .. n]
     hClose fh
```

Another way to write this would be to build a single large string, and then output that at once. There would then only by one function with a type involving **IO**, which we might consider cleaner.

5

The **IO** action built by the countLinesHandle function checks to see if we are at the end of the file. Then, there are no more lines, the result is 0. Otherwise we get one line, count the reset, and add one to the count. The **IO** action built by countLines function itself just deals with opening and closing the file.

```
countLinesHandle :: Num a ⇒ Handle → IO a
countLines :: Num a ⇒ FilePath → IO a

countLinesHandle fh =
  do e <- hIsEOF fh
     if e then return 0 else
        do hGetLine fh
           r <- countLinesHandle fh
           return (1 + r)

countLines filename =
  do fh <- openFile filename ReadMode
     lines <- countLinesHandle fh
     hClose fh
     return lines
```

6

The **IO** action built by copyFileHandle checks for the end of the input, then copies a line, and calls copyFileHandle again. The main function copyFile builds an **IO** action which opens the files in the appropriate modes, calls copyFileHandle, and closes the files again.

```
copyFileHandle :: Handle → Handle → IO ()
copyFile :: FilePath → FilePath → IO ()

copyFileHandle fromHandle toHandle =
  do e <- hIsEOF fromHandle
      if e then return () else
        do line <- hGetLine fromHandle
            hPutStrLn toHandle line
            copyFileHandle fromHandle toHandle

copyFile fromName toName =
  do fromHandle <- openFile fromName ReadMode
      toHandle <- openFile toName WriteMode
      copyFileHandle fromHandle toHandle
      hClose fromHandle
      hClose toHandle
```

7

Periods, exclamation marks and question marks may appear in multiples, leading to a wrong answer. The number of characters does not include newlines. It is not clear how quotations would be handled. Counting the words by counting spaces is inaccurate – a line with ten words will count only nine.

Chapter 15 (Building Bigger Programs)

1

First, we extend the Textstat module to allow frequencies to be counted and expose it through the interface, shown in Figure 15.3. Then the main program is as shown in Figure 15.4.

2

We can write two little functions which build **IO** actions – one to read all the lines from a file, and one to write them. The main **IO** action checks the command line to find the input and output file names, reads the lines from the input, reverses the list of lines, and writes them out. If the command is badly formed, it prints a usage message and exits. This is shown in Figure 15.5.

   Note that there is a problem if the file has no final newline – it will end up with one. How might you solve that?

3

See Figure 15.6. We use linesOfFile from Question 2, then map over the result to find the length of each line (remember strings are just lists of characters), then sum them. The result is printed to the screen.

```
module Textstat where

import System.IO

data Tree a = Br a (Tree a) (Tree a) | Lf deriving Show

type Stats = (Integer, Integer, Integer, Integer, Tree (Char, Integer))

(length', take', drop', filter', merge, mergeSort, listOfTree, treeLookup, and insert)

updateHistogram ::  (Ord a, Num b) => Tree (a, b) -> [a] -> Tree (a, b)

updateHistogram tr [] = tr
updateHistogram tr (x:xs) =
  case treeLookup tr x of
    Nothing ->
      updateHistogram (insert tr x 1) xs
    Just v ->
      updateHistogram (insert tr x (v + 1)) xs

statsFromChannel :: Handle -> Stats -> IO Stats

statsFromChannel fh (lines, characters, words, sentences, histogram) =
  do ended <- hIsEOF fh
     if ended then
       return (lines, characters, words, sentences, histogram)
     else
       do line <- hGetLine fh
          let charCount = length' line
              wordCount = length' (filter' (\x -> x == ' ') line)
              sentenceCount =
                length'
                  (filter'
                    (\x -> x == '.'|| x == '?'|| x == '!')
                    line)
          statsFromChannel
            fh
            (lines + 1, characters + charCount,
             words + wordCount, sentences + sentenceCount,
             updateHistogram histogram line)

statsFromFile :: FilePath -> IO Stats

statsFromFile filename =
  do fh <- openFile fileName ReadMode
     result <- statsFromChannel fh (0, 0, 0, 0, Lf)
     hClose fh
     return result
```

Figure 15.3: TextStat.hs

```
import System.Environment
import Textstat

(put our usual mergeSort and listOfTree functions here)

printHistogramList :: [(Char, Integer)] -> IO ()

printHistogramList [] = return ()
printHistogramList ((k, v):xs) =
  do putStr "For character "
     putStr (show k)
     putStr " the count is "
     putStr (show v)
     putStrLn "."
     printHistogramList xs

printHistogram :: Textstat.Tree (Char, Integer) -> IO ()

printHistogram tree =
  printHistogramList (mergeSort (listOfTree tree))

main :: IO ()

main =
  do args <- getArgs
     case args of
       [inFile] ->
         do (l, c, w, s, h) <- Textstat.statsFromFile inFile
            putStr "Lines: "
            putStrLn (show l)
            putStr "Characters: "
            putStrLn (show c)
            putStr "Words: "
            putStrLn (show w)
            putStr "Sentences: "
            putStrLn (show s)
        _ -> putStrLn "Usage: Stats <filename>"
```

Figure 15.4: `Stats.hs`

```
import System.Environment
import System.IO

(put our usual reverse' function here)

linesOfFile :: Handle -> IO [String]

linesOfFile fh =
  do finished <- hIsEOF fh
     if finished then return [] else
        do x <- hGetLine fh
           xs <- linesOfFile fh
           return (x : xs)

linesToFile :: Handle -> [String] -> IO ()

linesToFile _ [] = return ()
linesToFile fh (x:xs) =
  do hPutStrLn fh x
     linesToFile fh xs

reverseLines :: FilePath -> FilePath -> IO ()

reverseLines inFile outFile =
  do inHandle <- openFile inFile ReadMode
     outHandle <- openFile outFile WriteMode
     lines <- linesOfFile inHandle
     linesToFile outHandle (reverse' lines)
     hClose inHandle
     hClose outHandle

main :: IO ()

main =
  do args <- getArgs
     case args of
        [inFile, outFile] -> reverseLines inFile outFile
        _ -> putStrLn "Usage: RevLines input_filename output_filename"
```

Figure 15.5: `RevLines.hs`

```haskell
import System.Environment
import System.IO

(put our usual reverse', map', length' and sum' functions here)

linesOfFile :: Handle -> IO [String]

linesOfFile fh =
  do finished <- hIsEOF fh
     if finished then return [] else
       do x <- hGetLine fh
          xs <- linesOfFile fh
          return (x : xs)

numChars :: Num a => FilePath -> IO a

numChars inFile =
  do inHandle <- openFile inFile ReadMode
     lines <- linesOfFile inHandle
     hClose inHandle
     return (sum' (map' length' lines))

main :: IO ()

main =
  do args <- getArgs
     case args of
       [inFile] ->
         do size <- numChars inFile
            putStrLn (show size)
       _ ->
         putStrLn "Usage: Size filename"
```

Figure 15.6: `Size.hs`

4

See Figure 15.7. The meat of the solution is in `sortLines`. We must use `read` to read each number as an integer. Since we use read in conjunction with `map'`, the type annotation is on `read` itself, rather than the result of `read`, so it has a function type.

5

See Figure 15.8. It is a simple extension of our earlier function into a standalone program.

6

We can get all the lines in the file using `linesOfFile` from Question 2. The main **IO** action simply uses `matches` on each line, printing the line if `True` is returned.

The interesting function is `matches`. To see if `term` is in `line` we start at the beginning of the string, checking for a match. If a match is not found, we move on one position. This is illustrated in Figure 15.9.

```
import System.Environment
import System.IO

(put our usual reverse', map', merge, mergeSort, take', drop', and length' functions here)

linesOfFile :: Handle -> IO [String]

linesOfFile fh =
  do finished <- hIsEOF fh
     if finished then return [] else
       do x <- hGetLine fh
          xs <- linesOfFile fh
          return (x : xs)

linesToFile :: Handle -> [String] -> IO ()

linesToFile _ [] = return ()
linesToFile fh (x:xs) =
  do hPutStrLn fh x
     linesToFile fh xs

sortLines :: [String] -> [String]

sortLines lines =
  map' show (mergeSort (map' (read :: String -> Integer) lines))

sortNums :: FilePath -> FilePath -> IO ()

sortNums inFile outFile =
  do inHandle <- openFile inFile ReadMode
     outHandle <- openFile outFile WriteMode
     lines <- linesOfFile inHandle
     linesToFile outHandle (sortLines lines)
     hClose inHandle
     hClose outHandle

main :: IO ()

main =
  do args <- getArgs
     case args of
       [inFile, outFile] ->
         sortNums inFile outFile
       _ ->
         putStrLn "Usage: Size filename"
```

Figure 15.7: Sort.hs

```haskell
import System.Environment
import System.IO

copyFileHandle :: Handle -> Handle -> IO ()

copyFileHandle fromHandle toHandle =
  do e <- hIsEOF fromHandle
     if e then return () else
       do line <- hGetLine fromHandle
          hPutStrLn toHandle line
          copyFileHandle fromHandle toHandle

copyFile :: FilePath -> FilePath -> IO ()

copyFile fromName toName =
  do fromHandle <- openFile fromName ReadMode
     toHandle <- openFile toName WriteMode
     copyFileHandle fromHandle toHandle
     hClose fromHandle
     hClose toHandle

main :: IO ()

main =
  do args <- getArgs
     case args of
       [inFile, outFile] -> copyFile inFile outFile
       _ -> putStrLn "Usage: CopyFile in out"
```

Figure 15.8: `CopyFile.hs`

```haskell
import System.Environment
import System.IO
(put our usual reverse' and filter' functions here)

linesOfFile :: Handle -> IO [String]

linesOfFile fh =
  do finished <- hIsEOF fh
     if finished then return [] else
        do x <- hGetLine fh
           xs <- linesOfFile fh
           return (x : xs)

matches1 :: String -> String -> Bool

matches1 [] _ = True
matches1 _ [] = False
matches1 (x:xs) (y:ys) = x == y && matches1 xs ys

matches :: String -> String -> Bool

matches [] [] = True
matches _ [] = False
matches term (x:xs) = matches1 term (x : xs) || matches term xs

printStrings :: [String] -> IO ()

printStrings [] = return ()
printStrings (x:xs) =
  do putStrLn x
     printStrings xs

search :: FilePath -> String -> IO ()

search inFile searchString =
  do inHandle <- openFile inFile ReadMode
     lines <- linesOfFile inHandle
     let matched = filter' (matches searchString) lines
     printStrings matched
     hClose inHandle

main :: IO ()

main =
  do args <- getArgs
     case args of
       [inFile, searchString] -> search inFile searchString
       _ -> putStrLn "Usage: Search <file name> <search string>"
```

Figure 15.9: `Search.hs`

Chapter 16 (The Standard Prelude and Base)

1

The `Data.Char` module contains the function `toLower` which looks at a character and, if it is upper case, converts it to lower case. Otherwise the character is unaltered. We need only use `map` from the Standard Prelude to complete our tiny program:

```
process :: String → String

process s = map toLower s
```

Of course, we can simplify even further:

```
process :: String → String

process = map toLower
```

2

It is important to get the conditions exactly right.

```
isolate :: (Ord a, Num a) ⇒ [a] → [a]

isolate l =
   takeWhile (> 0) (dropWhile (<= 0) l)
```

Can you extend the function to return a list of all such positive series in a given list?

3

The word **otherwise** is simply defined as `True` in the Standard Prelude. Using **otherwise** simply makes our programs a little more pleasant to read.

4

The `Data.String` module contains the function `words` which splits a string into words, and `unwords` which does the reverse.

```
f :: String → String

f s = unwords (reverse (words s))
```

Here it is using the . operator:

```
f :: String → String

f = unwords . reverse . words
```

5

We can deduce that the numerical difference between each capital and lower case letter is 32:

GHCi:
Prelude> import Data.Char
Prelude Data.Char> ord 'a' - ord 'A'
32

So we may write our function, here using guarded equations:

```
toLower :: Char → Char

toLower c | c >= 'A' && c <= 'Z' = chr (ord c + 32)
          | otherwise = c
```

The number 32 seems like magic, though, and is harder to understand. We can use our earlier calculation directly:

```
toLower :: Char → Char

toLower c | c >= 'A' && c <= 'Z' = chr (ord c + ord 'a' - ord 'A')
          | otherwise = c
```

Hints for Questions

Chapter 1
Starting Off

1

Try to work these out on paper, and then check by typing them in. Can you show possible steps of evaluation for each expression?

3

Type it in. What does Haskell print? Consider the precedence of + and *.

5

What if a value of 2 appeared? How might we interpret it?

Chapter 2
Names and Functions

1

The function takes a number, and returns that number multiplied by ten. So what must its type be?

2

What does the function take as arguments? What is the type of its result? So what is the whole type? You can use the /= and && operators here.

3

What is the sum of all the integers from 1 . . . 1? Perhaps this is a good starting point.

4

This will be a recursive function. What happens when you raise a number to the power 0? What about the power 1? What about a higher power?

5

Can you define this in terms of the isVowel function we have already written?

6

Try adding parentheses to the expression in a way which does not change its meaning. Does this make it easier to understand?

7

When does it not terminate? Can you add a check to see when it might happen, and return 0 instead?

8

Which are expressions and which are function definitions? How many arguments does each function have? What typeclasses must each type variable belong to?

11

Remember that two types are equal if the type variables in one can be renamed to make the other.

Chapter 3
Case by Case

1

We are pattern matching on a boolean value, so there are just two cases: `True` and `False`.

2

Convert the **if** ... **then** ... **else** structure of the `sum'` function from the previous chapter into a pattern matching structure.

3

You will need three cases as before – when the power is 0, 1 or greater than 1 – but now in the form of a pattern match.

4

For the guarded equation version of `power`, we can begin `powerMatch x n | n ==` ...

5

Remember that characters may be compared using the comparison operators.

Chapter 4
Making Lists

1

Consider three cases: (1) the argument list is empty, (2) the argument list has one element, (3) the argument list has more than one element. In the last case, which element do we need to miss out?

2

The function will have type **Num** a $\Rightarrow$ **[Bool]** $\rightarrow$ a. Consider the empty list, the list with `True` as its head, and the list with `False` as its head. Count one for each `True` and zero for each `False`.

3

To detect if a list is a palindrome, consider the definition of a palindrome – a list which equals its own reverse.

4

Consider the cases (1) the empty list, (2) the list with one element, and (3) the list with more than one element.

5

Can any element exist in the empty list? If the list is not empty, it must have a head and a tail. What is the answer if the element we are looking for is equal to the head? What do we do if it is not?

6

The empty list is already a set. If we have a head and a tail, what does it tell us to find out if the head exists within the tail?

7

Consider in which order the ++ operators are evaluated in the reverse function. How long does each append take? How many are there?

9

Remember that x `rem` y == 0 if y is a factor of x.

10

The counting is not done as part of the list comprehension itself.

Chapter 5
Sorting Things

1

Consider adding another **let** before **let** left and **let** right.

2

Consider the situations in which `take'` and `drop'` can fail, and what arguments `mergeSort` gives them at each recursion.

3

This is a simple change – consider the comparison operator itself.

4

What will the type of the function be? Lists of length zero and one are already sorted – so these will be the base cases. What do we do when there is more than one element?

6

The **let** and **where** constructs can be used to introduce subsidiary functions, just as they can introduce other expressions.

Chapter 6
Functions upon Functions upon Functions

1

Recall that strings are really lists of characters. So the function `calm` is simple recursion on lists. There are three cases – the empty list, a list beginning with `'!'` and a list beginning with any other character. In the second part of the question, write a function `calmChar` which processes a single character. You can then use `map'` to define a new version of `calm`.

2

This is the same process as Question 1.

3

Look back at the section on anonymous functions. How can `clip` be expressed as an anonymous function? So, how can we use it with `map'`?

4

We want a function of the form `apply f n x = ...` which applies `f` to `x` a total of `n` times. What is the base case? What do we do in that case? What otherwise?

5

You will need to add the extra function as an argument to both `insert` and `sort` and use it in place of the `<=` operator in `insert`.

6

There are three possibilities: the argument list is empty, `True` is returned when its head is given to the function `f`, or `False` is returned when its head is given to the function `f`.

7

If the input list is empty, the result is trivially true – there cannot possibly be any elements for which the function does not hold. If not, it must hold for the first one, and for all the others by recursion.

8

You can use `map'` on each [a] in the [[a]].

9

Use the `filter'` function from Question 6, in addition to functions which reverse and sort lists.

Chapter 7
When Things Go Wrong

1

Make sure to consider the case of the empty list, where there is no smallest positive element, and also the non-empty list containing entirely zero or negative numbers.

2

We can pattern-match on the constructors `Just` and `Nothing` just like any other type.

3

First, write a function to find the number less than or equal to the square root of its argument. Now wrap up your function in another which, on a bad argument, gives zero or otherwise calls your first function. You can use the **where** construct to do this.

4

The type will be (a → **Maybe** b) → b → [a] → [b].

5

The type will be (a → **Either** b c) → [a] → ([b], [c]).

Chapter 8
Looking Things Up

1

The keys in a dictionary are unique – does remembering that fact help you?

2

The type will be the similar to (not the same as) the `add` function, but we only replace something if we find it there – when do we know we will not find it? What do we do if we cannot find it?

3

The function takes a list of keys and a list of values, and returns a dictionary. So it will have type [a] → [b] → [(a, b)]. Try matching on both lists at once – what are the cases?

4

This function takes a list of pairs and produces a pair of lists. So its type must be [(a, b)] → ([a], [b]). For the base case (the empty dictionary), we can see that the result should be ([], []). But what to

do in the case we have `(k, v):xs`? We must assign names for the two parts of the result of our function on `xs`, and then cons `k` and `v` on to them – can you think of how to do that? Perhaps using the **where** construct?

5

You can keep a list of the keys which have already been seen, and use the `elem'` function to make sure you do not add to the result list a key-value pair whose key has already been included.

6

The function will take two dictionaries, and return another – so you should be able to write down its type easily.

Try pattern matching on the first list – when it is empty, the answer is simple – what about when it has a head and a tail?

Chapter 9
More with Functions

2

Try building a list of booleans, each representing the result of `elem'` on a list.

3

The type of `map'` is (a → b) → [a] → [b]. The type of `mapl` is (a → b) → [[a]] → [[b]]. So, what must the type of `mapll` be? Now, look at our definition of `mapl` – how can we extend it to lists of lists of lists?

4

Use our `take'` function to process a single list. You may then use `map'` with this (partially applied) function to build the `truncateLists` function.

5

Build a function `firstElt` which, given the number and a list, returns the first element or that number. You can then use this function (partially applied) together with `map'` to build the main `firstElts` function.

6

Use `map'` to operate over each list in the list of lists.

Chapter 10
New Kinds of Data

1

The type will have two constructors: one for squares, requiring only a single number, and one for rectangles, requiring two: one for the width and one for the height. You will use the type variable `a` to represent the 'number', just like in the Colour type in the chapter text.

2

The function will have type **Num** a $\Rightarrow$ Rect a $\rightarrow$ a. Work by pattern matching on the two constructors of your type.

3

Work by pattern matching on your type. What happens to a square. What to a rectangle?

4

First, we need to rotate the rectangles as needed – you have already written something for this. Then, we need to sort them according to width. Can you use our `sort` function from Chapter 6 Question 5, which takes a custom comparison function?

5

Look at how we re-wrote `length'` and `append` for the Sequence type.

6

Add another constructor, and amend `evaluate` as necessary. You can use the `power` function from Chapter 2, Question 4.

Chapter 11
Growing Trees

1

The type will be **Eq** a $\Rightarrow$ a $\rightarrow$ Tree a $\rightarrow$ **Bool**. That is, it takes an element to search for, and a tree containing elements of the same type, and returns `True` if the element is found, and `False` if not. What happens if the tree is a leaf? What if it is a branch?

2

The function will have type Tree a $\rightarrow$ Tree a. What happens to a leaf? What must happen to a branch and its sub-trees?

3

If the two trees are both `Lf`, they have the same shape. What if they are both branches? What if one is a branch and the other a leaf or vice versa?

4

We have already written a function for inserting an element into an existing tree.

5

Try using list dictionaries as an intermediate representation. We already know how to build a tree from a list.

6

Consider using a list of sub-trees for a branch. How can we represent a branch which has no sub-trees?

Chapter 12
The Other Numbers

1

Use a pair to represent each coordinate. Ordinary arithmetic will do the rest.

2

Consider the type of the `ceiling` function. You may need `fromIntegral` here.

3

Consider the built-in function `floor`. What should happen in the case of a negative number? You may need `fromIntegral` here.

4

Calculate the column number for the asterisk carefully. How can it be printed in the correct column?

5

You will need to call the `star` function with an appropriate argument at points between the beginning and end of the range, as determined by the step.

6

Are **Bool** and **Char** in **Ord**? **Eq**? **Enum**? What about the numeric typeclasses?

Chapter 13
Being Lazy

1

This is very similar to `from` in the text.

3

Consider the definition of Fibonacci numbers. Split into a function which builds the list given two numbers, and the construction of the list itself.

4

We can use the tree type with just one constructor, `Br`, because leaves will never be needed.

5

The type of the function will be [a] → ([a], [a]). What are the base cases?

Chapter 14
In and Out

1

You may have to treat the last number in the list specially.

2

The `getIntegerMaybe` **IO** action from the chapter text is helpful here.

3

Ask the user the specify, beforehand, how many dictionary entries they are going to submit.

4

Begin with a function which builds an **IO** action to print a single row.

Chapter 15
Building Bigger Programs

3

Remember that a string is really just a list of characters.

4

The `read` function can be used to extract a number from each line of the file.

Chapter 16
The Standard Prelude and Base

4

The functions `words` and `unwords` are suitable.

5

How can we deduce the 'difference' between numbers assigned to lower case and upper case letters? Remember also that the comparison operators can be used on characters.

Coping with Errors

It is very hard to write even small programs correctly the first time. An unfortunate but inevitable part of programming is the location and fixing of mistakes. Haskell has a range of messages to help you with this process.

Here are descriptions of the common messages Haskell prints when a program cannot be accepted or when running it causes a problem (a so-called "run-time error"). We also describe warnings Haskell prints to alert the programmer to a program which, though it can be accepted for evaluation, might contain mistakes.

Errors before the program is run

These are messages printed when an expression could not be accepted for evaluation, due to being malformed in some way. No evaluation is attempted. You must fix the expression and try again.

Syntax errors

Syntax is the arrangement of letters and words and punctuation to make up sentences. In a programming language, a *syntax error* occurs when the arrangement is invalid and so its meaning cannot be determined. For example, if we use the wrong kind of quotation marks around the div operator:

```
Prelude> 1 'div' 2

<interactive>:1:3: error:
    • Syntax error on 'div'
      Perhaps you intended to use TemplateHaskell or TemplateHaskellQuotes
    • In the Template Haskell quotation 'div'
```

Notice that Haskell tries to tell us what we may have done wrong. In this case, the advice is incorrect, and indeed contains lots of words we do not understand. Such is the nature of error reporting in a programming language. The numbers :1:3: refer to the line and column number where the error occurs. For interactive programming this is of little help, but when compiling with ghc we can use the information to find the position in our text editor.

Reserved identifiers

Sometimes we inadvertently use a word which has a special meaning in Haskell, especially when we do not know the whole language:

```
GHCi:
Prelude> (class, teacher) = ("4b", "Mr Carter")
```

```
<interactive> error: parse error on input 'class'
```

These special words are printed in bold in this book. They are called reserved identifiers:

case class data default deriving do else
foreign if import in infix infixl infixr
instance let module newtype of then type where

Parse errors

This error occurs when Haskell finds that the program text contains things which are not valid words (such as **if**, **let** etc.) or other basic parts of the language, or when they exist in invalid combinations. These cause a failure to parse – the word parse means to read and understand the program's words. Check carefully and try again.

```
GHCi:
Prelude> 1 +
```

```
<interactive> error:
    parse error (possibly incorrect indentation or mismatched brackets)
```

For example, here we did not supply a right hand side for the addition operator.

Layout errors

The *layout rule*, introduced in Chapter 3, governs how Haskell constructs may be arranged spatially to make valid programs. The rule is simple to state, but easy to fall foul of, so the beginner is likely to be dealing with error messages arising from bad layout rather often. Sometimes Haskell correctly identifies the problem as a layout issue:

```
GHCi:
Prelude> :{
Prelude| sign x =
Prelude| if x < 0 then -1 else if x > 0 then 1 else 0
Prelude| :}
```

```
<interactive> error:
    parse error (possibly incorrect indentation or mismatched brackets)
```

Sometimes, however, Haskell cannot tell us that layout is the problem. You will get used to suspecting and fixing layout issues as a beginner.

Scope errors

This error occurs when you have mentioned a name which has not been defined (technically "bound to a value", or "in scope"). This might happen if you have mistyped the name.

```
GHCi:
Prelude> x + 1
```

```
<interactive> error: Variable not in scope: x
```

If the mistake is just a little one, Haskell may suggest the answer. In this case, `true` was probably not an undefined name, but a mistake for the defined constructor `True`:

```
GHCi:
Prelude> true

<interactive> error:
    • Variable not in scope: true
    • Perhaps you meant data constructor 'True' (imported from Prelude)
```

Data constructors can also be non-existent, causing an error:

```
GHCi:
Prelude> Blue

<interactive> error: Data constructor not in scope: Blue
```

Haskell knows it is an undefined data constructor rather than variable here, because it starts with a capital letter.

Type inference errors

One of the most common errors you will have to deal with as a Haskell programmer. For example:

```
GHCi:
Prelude> 1 + False

<interactive> error:
    • No instance for (Num Bool) arising from a use of '+'
    • In the expression: 1 + False
      In an equation for 'it': it = 1 + False
```

The error tells us that we cannot use a number on one side of the plus sign and a boolean on the other. Notice `Num` and `Bool` next to one another and the `'+'`. Often the error occurs late in the type inference mechanism, and so it can be hard to find the source of the error. Practice is all that helps here.

Sometimes, especially when compiling a program with `ghc`, we give both the type of a function and its definition. Haskell will infer the most general type for the function, and then compare with the type given, which may be more restrictive. If the type is less restrictive, or does not match at all, we see an error, and a suggested fix:

```
Prelude> :{
Prelude| f :: a -> a -> Bool
Prelude| f x y = x > y
Prelude| :}

<interactive> error:
    • No instance for (Ord a) arising from a use of '>'
      Possible fix:
        add (Ord a) to the context of
          the type signature for:
            f :: forall a. a -> a -> Bool
    • In the expression: x > y
      In an equation for 'f': f x y = x > y
```

In this case, the message suggests adding the **Ord** a constraint. The unary minus operator - can trip us up too:

```
Prelude> 2 * -x
```

```
<interactive> error:
    Precedence parsing error
        cannot mix '*' [infixl 7] and prefix '-' [infixl 6] in the same infix
        expression
```

Here, the solution is to parenthesize as (-x).

Warnings before a program is run

Warnings do not stop an expression being accepted or evaluated. They are printed after an expression is accepted but before the expression is evaluated. Warnings are for occasions where Haskell is concerned you may have made a mistake, even though the expression is not actually malformed. You should check each new warning in a program carefully.

Here is a warning that two pattern match cases overlap (in this case, they both match 0 so the second case cannot possibly be taken):

```
GHCi:
Prelude> :{
Prelude| f x =
Prelude|   case x of
Prelude|     0 -> 1
Prelude|     0 -> 2
Prelude| :}
```

```
<interactive> warning: [-Woverlapping-patterns]
    Pattern match is redundant
    In a case alternative: 0 -> ...
```

In addition, an error would occur upon evaluation if we called f with argument 1, because no case matches:

```
GHCi:
Prelude> f 1
*** Exception: <interactive>: Non-exhaustive patterns in case
```

The warning for this is not enabled by default, but starting ghci with argument -Wincomplete-patterns (or just -W to enable all warnings) adds this check:

```
<interactive> warning: [-Wincomplete-patterns]
    Pattern match(es) are non-exhaustive
    In a case alternative:
        Patterns not matched: a where a is not one of {0}
```

Errors when the program is run

In any programming language powerful enough to be of use, some errors cannot be detected before attempting evaluation of an expression (until "run-time"). For example, asking for the head of an empty list using the Standard Prelude's head function:

GHCi:
```
Prelude> head []
*** Exception: Prelude.head: empty list
```

We also saw such 'exceptions' when using read:

GHCi:
```
Prelude> read "16.5"
*** Exception: Prelude.read: no parse
Prelude> read "16.5" :: Integer
*** Exception: Prelude.read: no parse
```

These errors should be avoided by using functions which return types such as **Maybe** or **Either** like the readMaybe function.

Index

Printed in Great Britain
by Amazon

60907287R00122